Reflections of an Unconventional Mind

Reflections of an Unconventional Mind

Santishree Dhulipudi Pandit

KW Publishers Pvt Ltd
New Delhi

ISBN 978-81-982677-4-0 Hardback

Published in India by Kalpana Shukla

KW Publishers Pvt Ltd
4676/21, First Floor, Ansari Road
Daryaganj, New Delhi 110 002
Phone: +91 11 43528107
Marketing: kw@kwpub.in
Editorial: production@kwpub.in
Website: www.kwpub.in

Printed and bound in India

To

My father and teacher

Dhulipudi Anjaneyulu

With love, affection and admiration

Contents

Preface

In an era where ideological echo chambers often dictate narratives, this volume is an effort to explore the power of independent thought. This collection of essays represents an intellectual journey that challenges dominant discourses, interrogates historical distortions, and reclaims civilisational narratives from the clutches of ideological hegemony. Drawing from history, philosophy, politics, education, and contemporary global affairs, these essays are not just an academic exercise but a call to engage with ideas that shape our present and define our future.

The book is structured thematically, reflecting the diverse subjects that demand critical engagement. The sections on *History/Bhartiya Narratives* and *Icons* seek to shed light upon issues and individuals that remain out of the spotlight and, even worse, demonised over the years. These sections dismantle colonial and leftist distortions that have shaped Indian historiography, questioned the credibility of the Aryan Invasion Theory and critiqued the persistent attempts to impose a fractured vision of Bharat's past. Regarding the icons, the likes of Shivaji, Savarkar, and Ahilybai Holkar, among others, are covered. The section on *Indian Knowledge Systems (IKS)* underscores the need for decolonising education, exploring the role of Bharatiya traditions in shaping modern scientific and philosophical inquiry. A particular focus is given to contemporary debates surrounding the National Education Policy, the role of technology in higher education, and the importance of reclaiming India's intellectual traditions.

Nari Shakti brings to the fore the contributions of Indian women leaders and intellectuals, drawing attention to their role in shaping society. These essays move beyond tokenistic feminism to articulate a Bharatiya vision of women's empowerment rooted in history, agency, and self-determination. *Social Issues* find a critical voice in this collection, addressing challenges in the Northeast, Kashmir, and Manipur while exposing the manipulations of perception warfare in today's discourse. The volume also delves into *Foreign Policy*, offering a hard-hitting analysis of India's strategic challenges, the impact of terrorism as a geopolitical tool, and the emerging threats that seek to destabilise democracies worldwide.

At its core, this book is an assertion of civilisational confidence. It challenges the hegemonic discourse that seeks to define Bharat through an alien lens and instead offers a perspective deeply rooted in India's intellectual and philosophical traditions. In an age where cancel culture, ideological bias, and selective outrage dominate global discourse, the need for rigorous debate, fearless scholarship, and authentic storytelling has never been greater. This book is not an attempt to provide comfortable conclusions but an invitation to engage, question, and reimagine.

The essays featured here have been adapted from the author's weekly columns in *The Sunday Guardian* and occasional writeups in *The Indian Express* and *Hindustan Times*.

I extend my sincere appreciation to KW Publisher and its professional team, particularly Kalpana Shukla, Sanjeev Kumar Thakur, and Dharambir Singh, for their excellent work in copyediting, formatting, and the timely publication of this manuscript.

January 2025

Professor Santishree Dhulipudi Pandit
New Delhi, India

History/*Bharatiya* Narratives

1

Aryan Invasion Theory and Dravidian Distortions

Regardless of the domain, a theory is never considered the final word; it remains subject to criticism and debunking as the theories are just conjectures. The Aryan Invasion Theory (AIT) is one such conjecture in history that stands out as one of the most flawed and divisive interpretations of the *Bharatiya* civilisation and its rich history. For these reasons, the theory is increasingly treated with scepticism and disdain due to its lack of academic rigor and its ideological agenda. Moreover, other critical factors that have caused the theory to lose credibility include the availability of archaeological evidence that has debunked the theory and an increasing public interest in discovering the truth about India's past, which has long been narrated by outsiders with vested interests. Unfortunately, the theory still lingers in small yet vocal circles of left-leaning academics and intellectuals who view it as a potent tool for dividing people based on the concepts of race, caste and religion, which is based on faulty assumptions and prejudiced conjectures.

This theory has given rise to the faulty construct of a divide between Aryans and Dravidians by Bishop Robert Caldwell, whose primary purpose in his Colonial/Church agenda. Surprisingly, this false conjecture was constructed on Aryan invasions that never took place. This is the mainstay of the 'distorians' of the Dravidian parties. Rationalism and atheism are anti-all religion, but the hypocrisy of these parties is that many of them are faithful to *Abrahamic faiths* and attack only Hinduism. Hence, should one conclude that the Dravidian parties are the followers of Caldwell's Colonial, Church, and Conversion construct and are contributing Hinduphobia? Recent archaeological excavations at Rakhigarhi, Dwarka and many other places have proved by carbon dating that we are 8,000 to10,000 years old. The geological theories indicate the lost lands at the end of the Ice Age due to massive flooding especially in the Indian peninsula. So, we were civilised when Europe and the West were still in the primitive stages. We were an outward civilisation. We civilised them and not the reverse. Science and evidence disprove all these divisive conjectures constructed for the Colonial Church Conversion Project. Why are we still perpetuating the same?

A Fallacious Theory

The AIT (also referred to as the Indo-Aryan migration theory), often championed by leftist historians, constitutes a part of a broader theoretical framework aimed at diminishing the historical significance of the ancient *Bharatiya* civilisation by attributing its establishment to an external race depicted as invaders. This theoretical perspective seeks to leverage linguistic connections among various contemporary and ancient languages, interpretations derived from philology, and findings from archaeological and anthropological research. This colonial endeavour reduced the millennia-old developments in the subcontinent to the imagined notions of race that colonial powers believed in and employed during their imperial conquests. Also worth mentioning is the pernicious Aryan-Dravidian divide that the AIT encouraged and propagated by figures like Caldwell, with his Comparative Grammar of Dravidian Languages and Bishop Campbell in the mid-19th century. This divisive narrative aimed to segregate Indian society along racial and caste lines, thus the sowing seeds of division.

Erroneous to the Core

The Aryan invasion theory has indeed been criticised endlessly for its flawed assumptions and ideologically driven agenda that transposed colonial ideas and racial divides onto the Indian subcontinent. The theory has been used to legitimise British colonialism in India by proposing a fallacious disposition that suggests Aryans colonised India. This narrative could arguably be seen as an effort to justify or normalise the British presence and actions in India by drawing parallels with an alleged ancient Aryan colonisation. Moreover, the theory seems to deflect colonial blame and shame from British shoulders. By suggesting that Aryans were historical colonisers, the theory sought to argue that Britain was not doing anything different from what India had seen in the past. In other words, the theory served as an attempt to diffuse the criticism of British colonialism by asserting that even Indians were guilty of colonisation and, therefore, Indians under British rule should accept British suzerainty without complaint.

In addition to the evident harm caused by such a pernicious theory, it is crucial to highlight the implicit strategies employed by the British to normalise it as the ultimate and unquestionable truth. As part of their so-called educational reforms aimed at undermining and demotivating the young populace of India, the British actively promoted the theory in schools and colleges. The relentless dissemination of the theory, without presenting credible evidence, critical viewpoints, or alternative perspectives, led individuals of that time to accept it at face value. While the British, guided by their colonial interests, bear responsibility for these actions, perhaps more significant blame has to be assigned to leftist intellectuals and historians who played an essential role in perpetuating this divisive narrative post-independence.

Leftist Embrace of AIT

A distorted mentality has influenced the propagation and spread of the AIT, particularly after leftist ideologies gained prominence in India in the early 20th century and solidified under the Nehruvian government post-independence. During this period, the AIT and the Aryan-Dravidian schism were embraced with enthusiasm by the left, providing them with a tool to foster division, turning communities against one another and ushering in self-inflicted hate towards their ancestors and history. As a result, a complex Indian consciousness emerged in the mid-20th century when numerous Indians began to harbour disdain for their history and origins. Essentially, these leftist historians, wielding authoritative control over narratives, inherited and continued the interpretative legacy left by the British. Their influence further exacerbated existing divides by propagating views that kept the country fragmented. The authoritarian control over historical narratives allowed these scholars to shape and disseminate perspectives that reinforced divisive notions, contributing to the fragmentation of the Indian identity.

What remains most encouraging in discussions on the AIT and the Aryan-Dravidian divide is the transformed academic environment that today's India provides, where such fallacious theories and misrepresentations are countered and debunked through facts, evidence, and logic. Recent archaeological excavations at Rakhigarhi, Dwarka, and Keeladi have systematically dismantled myths surrounding these erroneous theories. In the spirit of Prime Minister Narendra Modi's speech at the Ram Mandir Pran Pratishta (2024), where he united Indians under the banner of development and progress and urged citizens to 'lay the foundation for the next thousand years of Bharat', this foundation must be built on high intellectual traditions free of ideology, sycophancy, and falsehoods. Uprooting and debunking theories like the AIT is a crucial part of this effort, and the youth must take the lead in challenging colonial- assumptions and narratives that have beleaguered India for so long. A genuine history of *Bharatiya* civilisation, rooted in truth and evidence, is the precursor to realising the vision of *Viksit Bharat* (Developed India), which is a saga of continuity with change, realm with region, diversity and unity, tradition with modernity, balance with chaos, spiritual with the material— a holistic vision for all from the unique to the universal and the cosmos.

2

'Integral Humanism' for Contemporary Bharat

The Nehruvian State and its policy of cancel culture systematically marginalised and branded several Indian thinkers as communal when they were, in fact, the opposite. Many, like Aurobindo, Tilak, Ambedkar, Savarkar and Deendayal Upadhyay, were pushed out of the mainstream without serious study. Now, the time has come to correct this bias of the Left and Wokes and it is necessary to seriously study the contributions of these *Bharatiya* thinkers to help build an alternative narrative. These individuals were the organic intellectuals who led the counter-cultural revolution.

India's Rich Political Philosophy

While figures like Chanakya and his *Arthashastra*, as well as the ideas of Vivekananda or Dayanand Saraswati's Arya Samaj, do garner recognition, in the broader context of great thinkers and philosophers of India, they amount to a mere drop in the ocean. The asymmetry in discourse highlights a Western-centric focus within the academic and intellectual spheres, overshadowing the rich political philosophies that have emerged from the East. In the post-Independence era, the discourse on political thought has largely dried up, with an irresistible focus on Nehruvian ideology that even overshadows Gandhian philosophy.

This has led some to lament the 'poverty of Indian political theory'. Be that as it may, the Independence struggle witnessed a revival of philosophical and political ideas drawing upon the ancient traditions of Sanatan Dharma. Undeniably, the philosophical contributions of figures such as Lajpat Rai, Bose, Tilak, Bipin Chandra, Savarkar, Bharatiyar, Golwalkar, Aurobindo, RC Majumdar, and Shyama Prasad Mukherji profoundly impacted on the society and the Indian psyche, playing a pivotal role in propelling the Independence Movement from the grassroots.

What made these ideas particularly striking was their grounding in the reality of India and their deep-rooted connection to Bharat's historical traditions and cultural values. Deendayal Upadhyaya's (25 September 1916 to 11 February 1968) Integral Humanism' stands out as a significant contribution that redefined *Bharatiya* traditions within modern political systems, emphasising the synthesis of traditional values with contemporary political thought.

Integral Humanism: An Indian Philosophy

The ideas encapsulated in Integral Humanism are distilled from Deendayal Upadhyaya's years of experience, particularly his work with the Jan Sangh and interactions with numerous individuals, mainly between 1959 and 1964. What emerged was a philosophy authentically Indian, woven into the fabric of national rejuvenation movements that aspired to shape the future of India as a nation, society, and humanity at large.

Though Upadhyaya's ideas were cut short by his untimely passing, they remarkably established the foundational parameters of thought that remain profoundly relevant even today. At its core, this philosophy advocates disavowing dialecticism and the integration of *Vyasthi* (Individual), *Samasthi* (Society), *Srishti* (Creation), and *Parameshti* (Creator).

These are not merely philosophical values but also extend into the realm of politics. The goals of a nation and its society must find their roots in the natural pursuits of Dharma, Artha, Kama, and Moksha. This requires a retrospective examination of the past, delving into the treasures of philosophical, political, and social significance throughout Indian history, including the contributions of figures such as Shankaracharya. In such a sense, Upadhyaya's views emphasise the importance of civilisational and cultural nationalism, asserting that these concepts predate the West's perspectives on Westphalian statehood.

Disavowing Dialecticism

The ideas of the West, whether on the Right or Left, are rooted in binaries of 'us vs. them'. They revolve around differences and conflicts between two opposing aspects: individual vs. group, nature vs. humans, and spirituality vs. secularism. The dualist nature of these ideas compels readers and practitioners to choose between two opposite sides, a concept that proves inapplicable when closely examining Indian history.

Even the more recent debates on capitalism vs. socialism and welfare vs. utilitarian state are entangled in this binary thinking. In his significant work, Upadhyaya urges us to rise above the individualistic and dialectical conclusions that most Western-originated ideas propagate. Instead, he advocates for integrating and including these diverse themes and views into a syncretic form, where the church and state coexist harmoniously under the concept of Dharma. The pursuit is for wholesomeness, countering the ideas of alienation and separation, merging the experiences of the soul and the physical being.

Contemporary Relevance

Pursuing the goal of resembling the West in its purest form is a dangerously predisposed inclination. The threats of Wokeness and unchecked liberal values are steering the West towards an abyss of unimaginable magnitude. Traditional values tied to family, kinship, marriage, and society are sacrificed on the altar of individualism, masking the abandonment of personal responsibility in favour of self-gratification and identity politics.

This has fostered conflicts and greater polarisation, resulting in an increased tendency towards violence within societies. Upadhyaya's Integral Humanism emerges as a solution to these pressing problems. His vision of merging nature with development and intertwining individual rights and responsibilities with societal and national duties provides us with an enlightening guide for leading a life that is meaningful and beneficial to those around us. Crucially, we cannot and should not forsake our religious and spiritual values for the pursuit of an atheistic interpretation of secularism.

As we see, what often passes for secularism in India is not the separation of religion and politics but rather a lack of understanding and ignorance of religion. Thus, what holds significance is the positioning of humans in the grand scheme of things and how they should conduct themselves to foster a society and nation that is inclusive and forward-looking.

The imperative is not for a conflict between nature and humans but for a quest for harmony. This is why all rivers, mountains, and organic elements around us are accorded the status of gods and goddesses. Ancient wisdom recognised their value and greatness in sustaining us, emphasising that our actions cannot exist independently of our surroundings. They must be harmonious with our ecosystem, where material development is pursued respectfully alongside a quest for spirituality.

The prevailing problems of alienation and disenchantment that seem to permeate every segment of human life today are ominous signals that demand sincere and concerted efforts. The philosophy of Integral Humanism serves as the instrument to achieve that balance and harmony. The integration of *Vyasthi, Samasthi, Srishti*, and *Parameshti* points the way forward. A contemporary revolution in Indian consciousness unfolds through realising and acknowledging our rich traditions and cultural wealth. We need to disseminate such ideas and develop them further to set us on a path of enlightenment that is not solely materialistic or individualistic but spiritual and filled with *anand* (joy).

3

How Science Exposes the Left 'Distorians'

"Power is knowledge."

– Michael Foucault

"The AIT (Aryan Invasion Theory) is based purely on linguistic conjectures which are unsubstantiated."

– Klostermaier, *A Survey of Hinduism*, 2007, p. 21.

The National Education Policy (NEP 2020) has raised the aspirations of all stakeholders, calling for the pursuit of a holistic architecture of knowledge. The most important being how the nationalist epistemic community is going to construct the *Bharatiya* narrative architecture. The Left and Nehruvians cleverly followed the policies of the invaders and the colonials. While the Islamist iconoclasts directly attacked temples, looted, plundered and committed rape, the British were more cunning as they systematically lowered the values of these holy cities within the state machinery and the commercial empire they built. And these false conjectures have been embedded into textbooks at all levels.

Advances in science and the tools it provides exposed false interpretations. Two such archaeological excavations—Rakhigarhi and Keeladi—have demolished two major myths they constructed: One the Aryan invasion/migration theory and the Aryan/Dravidian divide, or the North-South divide.

Rakhigarhi is a village and an archaeological site belonging to the Indus Valley civilisation in the Hisar district of Haryana State, situated about 150 km northwest of Delhi. It was part of the mature phase of the Indus Valley civilisation, dating to 2600-1900 BCE. The Aryan invasion theory, also referred to as the Indo-Aryan migration theory by leftist historians, has been debunked. Also called the Indo-Aryan migration theory, it is part of a larger theoretical framework of downgrading the Ancient Indic Civilisation by claiming it was established by invaders. This framework attempts to explain the similarities between a wide range of contemporary and ancient languages. It combines linguistic, archaeological and anthropological research. This provides an overview of the development of Indo-European languages, and the spread of these Indo-European languages by migration and acculturation. This was a colonial project.

The research—published in Cell, one of the world's top journals—not only sets aside the Aryan migration theory but also notes that the hunter-gatherers of Southeast Asia transitioned into farming communities on their own and were the ancestors of the Harappan population. It demolishes the hypothesis of mass human migration during Harappan time from outside South Asia or before, said VS Shinde, an archaeologist at Deccan College Post-Graduate and Research Institute in Pune and one of the lead authors of the study. The Rakhigarhi samples do show traces of genes of Iranian lineage. However, the antiquity of these genes dates back 11,000 to 12,000 years, far before the Harappan civilisation. Since 7000 BCE, there is no evidence of the South Asian genes being mixed with Central Asian genes. "Research showed the Vedic culture was developed by the indigenous people of South Asia," Shinde asserted. The knowledge of agriculture was also indigenous as the pre-historic hunter-gatherer learnt how to do farming.

Neeraj Rai, a scientist at the Birbal Sahani Institute of Paleobotany, Lucknow, said the research also pointed towards an 'Out of India' theory around 2500-3000 BCE. The evidence comes from a related study by the same set of researchers, published simultaneously in the journal Science on Friday. The Rakhigarhi woman's genome matched those of 11 other ancient people who lived in what is now Iran and Turkmenistan, at sites known to have exchanged objects with the Indus Valley Civilisation. All 12 had a distinctive mix of ancestry, including a lineage related to Southeast Asian hunter-gatherers and an Iranian-related lineage specific to South Asia. The Indus Valley Civilisation, which at its height from 2600 to 1900 BCE covered a large swath of northwestern South Asia, was one of the world's first large-scale urban societies.

IIT Kharagpur released its 2022 calendar, titled 'Recovery of the Foundations of Indian Knowledge Systems', which includes various topics, some of which are controversial and likely to raise some hackles 'Why an Aryan invasion myth was forged' (September 2022). Some of the reactions on social media were negative regarding the topics chosen and some 'mistakes' were pointed out based on primarily ideological differences. All those who were completely okay for many years with distortions and false information being fed to children and adults alike in the name of history, are suddenly raising their voices upon seeing actual historical data and evidence being presented to the common people.

Keeladi could also provide crucial evidence for understanding the missing links of the Iron Age (12th Century BCE to 6th Century BCE) and the Early Historic Period (6th Century BCE to 4th Century BCE) and subsequent cultural developments. The similarity of the Tamil Brahmi script to the Indus Valley Brahmi script indicates that the inhabitants of the Indus Valley were those who migrated, contrary to the reverse being suggested. The great Indian divide along north-south lines now appears blurred. A pathbreaking study by Harvard and indigenous researchers on ancestral Indian populations suggests there is a genetic relationship among all Indians and more importantly, the hitherto believed 'fact' that Aryans and Dravidians represent the ancestry of North and South Indians, might after all, be a myth.

'This paper rewrites history... there is no north-south divide," Lalji Singh, former director of the Centre for Cellular and Molecular Biology (CCMB) and a co-author of the study concluded.

Senior CCMB scientist Kumarasamy Thangarajan stated there was no truth to the Aryan-Dravidian theory as they emerged hundreds or thousands of years after the ancestral North and South Indians had settled in India. The study analysed 500,000 genetic markers across the genomes of 132 individuals from 25 diverse groups across 13 states. All the individuals were from six-language families and traditionally 'upper' and 'lower' castes and tribal groups. "The genetics indicate that castes grew directly out of tribe-like organisations during the formation of Indian society", the study said. Thangarajan noted that it was impossible to distinguish between castes and tribes since their genetics indicated they were not systematically different.

A holistic and interdisciplinary approach has exposed the Nehruvian-Left lobby, who manufactured history and narratives for some persons and purposes.

4

Wokeism and the Preferential Manipulation of Identity

The Presidents of US Ivy league universities', all women, shamelessly defended their inaction against those who called for the genocide of Jews on their campuses. The three major universities—Harvard University, University of Pennsylvania and the Massachusetts Institute of Technology (MIT)—were questioned by the US Congress about anti-Semitism on their campuses, which threatens the lives of Jewish students.

They cut such a sorry figure with their diversionary answers. Instead of a straight 'No', all replied with riders and caveats. This is because of where they come from—their radicalised Woke mentality which makes them think that they are progressive. In their mental construct, certain communities are the permanent oppressors—despite historical facts saying otherwise—like Jews and Hindus, while the permanent victims are Blacks and Muslims. Anybody who supports these so-called imagined oppressors are in for trouble.

Public institutions and top universities in Europe and America have supported the 'cancel culture' where words must be translated into conduct and action applied selectively. Cancel culture has consistently maintained that words constitute violence if they do not align with the identities they support like Blacks and Muslims.

This they have exported abroad and one can see an abundance of this in public space and university campuses in India as well. Social media contributes to these imagined constructs and absurdities where calls to genocide can be mainstreamed by people. Worse, they believe they are acting with good in intentions. Women's rights do not matter compared to those whom they support.

Hamas broke the pact earlier than planned on the eighth day when ten young women were supposed to be released. US State Department spokesperson Mathew Miller commented that probably Hamas did not want to turn over these women because they feared that they may speak about what happened to them during their time in custody.

The silence of the UN, women's rights organisations and the so called Wokes is shocking. Women have been raped, sexually abused and mutilated by these terrorists and yet there has been no condemnation.

Why is it so—Is it because these women do not belong to the identities that the Wokes community supports? Has the UN become so Woke that it no longer represents everyone? A weak and feeble condemnation came after two months, which is ineffective, as it is too little, too late.

The blatant catering to the bigots done in the name of sensitivity and permanent victimhood—even if they are the real oppressors, is an imagined construct based on a false consciousness. The situation is such that one cannot speak of Armenian or Hindu genocide in history or even in recent times.

In fact, Wokeism undermines the traditional tenets of the Left, it prioritises tribal dogma over universal commitments and undermines the hope of progress itself. Wokeism begins with the concern for the marginalised individuals, but ends up reducing each person to the prism of their marginalisation.

The idea of intersectionality was once a useful reminder that each of us has multiple identities. But now, it leads to a narrow focus on the most marginalised aspects and turns them into a 'forest of trauma'.

The proponents of Wokeism are so caught up in inequalities of power and culture wars that they have forgotten how to unite in the struggle for justice. Wokeism reduces our complex identities to the narrow axes of race, gender (or caste or sexual orientation) alone, and fixates on the idea that only those exactly like us can be our allies.

It is assumed that our social position determines our claim to knowledge—only a woman can know this, only a person with disabilities can understand this, and so on. But victimhood alone confers no virtue. The valorisation of one's trauma leads to self-expression, but not to social change.

One must fight the social fictions of race, caste and gender with common ideals, not identities. How, then, does social and political change happen? When we build coalitions, when people rally together across gender, caste and race, and other identities, for the sake of their convictions.

Even the white individuals or upper-caste people who marched for Black Lives Matter or caste annihilation did so out of a commitment to universal justice. Tribal thinking reduces everything to self-interest and frustrates the possibility of egalitarian movements. It mirrors the identity politics of conservatives.

Woke movements tend to tear down enlightenment ideas of universal liberal ideals, reason, progress and so on, arguing that it is the Eurocentric ideology that justified colonial predations by the West. They point out (rightly) that 'universal' is often coded as white rather than brown, male rather than female, and straight rather than gay. However, this book argues that enlightenment thinkers instilled a guilty conscience regarding colonialism, something that older 'might is right' empires never had.

Those who once identified as being on the Left, now refer to themselves progressive, yet they undermine any hope for progress. To be on the left is to stand behind the idea that people can work together to create real change in their own lives and those of others. Woke theories possess an implacable doomsday logic that renders reform seem futile. They miss how things have got better on racial issues, gender equality, on confronting our pasts.

Sexual harassment was once considered like the weather, now, it is at least condemned and actionable, even if it remains pervasive, as in the case of the Hamas. Wokeism is largely confined to squabbling on social media over what discrimination is worse, rather than building solidarity across our differences. The personal is political, certainly, but when the political is reduced to only the personal, we lose hope. It is time to return to the universal.

5

Imagined Histories in Independent India

Imagined histories produce agenda-setting and biased interpretations. Caste has been used and abused as both a term and a category of analysis. It is not confined to one faith but exists in every faith, especially in South Asia, where it stands out prominently. Are we more casteist for seeking political and economic benefits? The dream of the greatest Indian, Babasaheb Dr BR Ambedkar, who was marginalised by those in power until 2014 is one we need to take very seriously today. The Left and Liberal academia avoided him because he was very critical of their hypocrisy. At best, they praised a select few who were in power and helped them to exercise authority without ever winning elections. There are major gaps in the writing of Indian history where, by design or intention, there has been a clear attempt to agenda set in favour of a Republican dynasty, which continues to dominate textbooks and publicly funded institutions. Are we suggesting that only one family won us freedom while all the others who sacrificed their lives have been marginalised?

One such historical icon, BR Ambedkar, critically analysed and fought for the annihilation of caste. By pursuing true and original thinking, he followed Brahma-vidyaand, as per the scriptures, was a true Brahmin in the Vedic sense, a person who pursues and produces knowledge. There is ample evidence that the seminal Hindu texts were written by Valmiki (Ramayana), Vyasa (Mahabharata), and BR Ambedkar, the architect of our Constitution and a lot of his writings. On 26 November, we all celebrated the Constitution Day and reaffirmed our faith in its Preamble, which embodies liberty, equality and fraternity to all. On 6 December, we observe Mahanirvana Diwas, the day we lost this great thinker, the tallest Indian and Modern India's icon. In the idea of dissent that Lord Gautama the Buddha was the first dissenter of the *Bharatiya* tradition to Babasaheb. We celebrate dissent and diversity in our *Bharatiya* tradition through *Ekam Sat Vipraha Bahuda Vadanti* (Truth is one; the wise call it by various names). They warned of the social evils that have crept in into an inclusive and diverse *parampara* or tradition.

All political parties in India are caste-ridden, even the Left. Left liberals among the academia practice it more vigorously, though engage in a lot of doublespeak. Unfortunately, the social sciences have refused to take a thinker like BR Ambedkar seriously. Why? Any discussion of law in India and abroad must include and begin with one of the strongest proponents of the rule of law, the father of our Constitution, BR Ambedkar. He, a visionary leader and the chief architect of the Indian Constitution, held a nuanced perspective on the intersection of law and economics, particularly in pursuing social justice and uplifting marginalised communities. Many of his insights, while not always captured verbatim in quotes, can be extrapolated from his extensive writings and speeches.

He famously noted, "Political democracy cannot last unless there lies at the base of it social democracy. What does social democracy mean? It means a way of life that recognises liberty, equality, and fraternity as the principles of life." Dr Ambedkar's concern for economic inequality was deeply ingrained in his philosophy. He went beyond guaranteeing political rights, advocating for legal frameworks that would actively contribute to addressing economic disparities. In his vision, a just society required not only political and social equality but also economic parity.

In pursuit of economic equality, Ambedkar championed the cause of land reforms. He recognised that the equitable distribution of land was pivotal for empowering the marginalised sections of society. His conviction lay in the belief that without addressing economic disparities at the grassroot level, the lofty ideals of democracy would remain incomplete. One of Ambedkar's notable stances was his emphasis on labour rights and fair wages. He saw protecting workers' rights as a fundamental step towards achieving economic justice. For him, the toiling masses—those who tilled the soil, cultivated raw materials, and created goods—were indispensable contributors to the production and distribution of wealth.

Ambedkar's vision of a just society was intricately woven into the fabric of economic empowerment. He recognised that the quest for social justice would be incomplete without dismantling exploitative labour practices and ensuring fair economic opportunities. While specific quotes capturing these sentiments directly may be limited, delving into his seminal works, such as *Annihilation of Caste*, and examining his contributions to the framing of the Indian Constitution provide a richer understanding of Ambedkar's profound views on the symbiotic relationship between law and economics in the pursuit of a fair and inclusive society.

Today some people are calling for a caste census, which is ironic given that our history is full of individuals who fought and struggled to make caste disappear from society. What never ceases to captivate me is the resilience and foresight embedded in our Constitution, a testament to the brilliance of its creators, including the visionary BR Ambedkar. In an era witnessing myriad changes across sectors, including the emergence of previously non-existent ones, our Constitution continues to adapt and keep pace with evolving times. Emerging concerns, such as environmental issues and sustainability, have now assumed central importance. Surprisingly, the concept of sustainability, championed in recent decades, finds its roots in the foresight of Indian lawmakers, including the visionary BR Ambedkar, dating back to the 1950s. This early endorsement highlights the enduring relevance of sustainable principles, demonstrating remarkable prescience on the part of Ambedkar and his contemporaries.

Promoting diversity and inclusivity within the legal sphere, encompassing jurisprudence and law practice, is paramount. Such inclusivity ensures a more comprehensive understanding of the multifaceted challenges posed by evolving technologies, fostering a legal landscape that is not only adept but also reflective of the diverse society it serves. As underscored in his extensive writings, Ambedkar illuminated a crucial truth: a nation's development remains incomplete until every individual, irrespective of their station in life, reaps its benefits. The recent milestone achievement of India—soaring to a US$4 trillion economy—is undoubtedly cause for celebration. Successes like these are not just the triumph of economic numbers but a testament to a society embracing a more inclusive and equitable distribution of resources—a journey championed by many stalwarts over the years.

6

Doublethink, Doublespeak and Dystopia

What greatly surprises anyone observing the Israel-Hamas war is that Marxists/Wokes are aligning with the Islamists and using their tactics of cancel culture against those who dissent. Is there something much deeper to this collaboration between groups that ideologically can never come together. It is an oxymoron. How is an objective scholar to view this collaboration? Karl Marx stated that religion is the opium of the masses and Raymond Aron claimed that Marxism is the opium of intellectuals. Now the Woke's support the terrorists who have hijacked religion to annihilate the Jews, forgetting that Marx himself was Jewish. What a paradox. One is intrigued by a surge of demonstrations for ceasefire, which will benefit terror groups like Hamas which is on the defensive to re-group. Both Russia and China have fought Islamist terror with an iron hand and they have denied them their cultural rights domestically. Where were these Wokes/and the Islamists then? This is doublespeak in a dystopian world.

Dystopia, also called a cacotopia or anti-utopia, is a speculative community or society that is undesirable or frightening. Dystopias are often characterised by fear or distress of tyrannical governments or other characteristics associated with a cataclysmic decline in society. According to Winston Smith, the protagonist of *1984*, doublethink is to know and not to know, to be conscious of complete truthfulness while telling carefully constructed lies, to hold simultaneously two opinions which cancel each other out, knowing them to be contradictory and believing in both of them, to use logic against. Doublethink may occur because of someone being wilfully perverse or as a result of faulty logic. The term 'Doublethink' was coined by George Orwell for the novel *1984*. Doublespeak is the use of euphemistic or ambiguous language in order to disguise what one is actually saying. Orwell uses the irony of doublethink to show how manipulation and control can restrict one's individuality and freedom and creating a mob psychology.

The unfortunate truth is that the in the Israel-Hamas war, the left and the Wokes, instead of discussing the war and the reason behind *jihadist* terror are attacking the Other—the victims: the Jews, Christians and Hindus. In India the Woke brigade in academia, funded by international and national global corporate interests are attacking Jews, Hinduism, and Hindutva. Is this not academic doublethink and doublespeak? Attacking Hindus is the easiest for they do not retaliate by beheading as seen in the case of the cartoons and Charlie Hebdo. It is fear of indiscriminate violence that prevents anyone from daring to confront *jihadist* terror for fear of retaliation. Hence, we see the glorification and legitimation of *Jihadist* terror. For the Left, the means of *Jihadi* terror do not matter as long as the end is achieved by whatever means—loot, plunder, rape, murder. That makes them strange bedfellows. Why this doublethink and doublespeak?

Are we in an Orwellian world of Dystopia where war is peace and ignorance is strength. Doublethink is the power of holding two contradictory beliefs in one's mind simultaneously, and accepting both of them. Rape, looting, murder, torture, and plunder, but the faith is portrayed as peaceful. The Left and the Wokes are against religion but not the Islamists and *jihadi* terror. This is indeed doublethink, doublespeak and dystopia.

In the land of the birth of Islam, Saudi Arabia, there are no protests supporting Hamas terrorists, nor in many Arab states. Most of these countries do not accept Palestinian refugees. The journey of the Palestinian struggle is from the secular romance of Yasir Arafat of resistance and his PLO and Fatah party to the savage and fanatical iteration of *jihadi* terrorism of the Hamas which many in the Arab states also condemn. Prince Turki al-Faisal, the former intelligence chief of Saudi Arabia, speaking at Rice University's Baker Institute (Houston) stated, "I prefer the other option: civil insurrection and disobedience. It brought down the British Empire in India and the Soviet empire in Eastern Europe."

Here is another glaring example of doublethink and doublespeak. Moussa Abu Marzouk, head of Hamas' international relations office in Doha, Qatar, speaking to *Frontline* and in response to a question on Hamas killing Israeli civilians on October 7 said: "There are also Israeli testimonies that those who killed Israeli civilians were their army because the army bombed the houses surrounding the fighters, killing dozens of civilians, and the extent of the destruction proves that it was at Israeli hands. Our fighters had light weapons and armoured vehicle shells. As for the music festival, used by Israeli propaganda to claim that Hamas killed them [the people attending it], we did not know that there was a festival in that area."

"The Israeli army and security services arrived at the celebration before the fighters arrived there to evacuate them, so the area became a military zone, and clashes occurred. Also, according to the confessions of some Israelis witnesses, the Israeli army killed many civilians when it fired missiles." *Frontline*, the mouthpiece of the Wokes in India, did not even consider of cross checking or contesting such statements as part of objectivity and fair play.

In the age of Hamas, morality has become a part of the progressive pieties in which the motif of victimisation continues to be culturally updated, atrocity by atrocity. The jargon of insensitivity pretends to represent a moral position. The tyranny of phrases like Islamophobia seeks to divert attention from the fundamental right to life and land, and creates a doctrine of false consciousness and victimhood out of a staggering mathematics of the dance of rape, loot, murder and death.

Today, the Wokes and Islamists have been the party which is always right. Aron's prediction can rightly be applied to the Woke, who are 'convinced that it acts with a view to achieving the only future, that is worthwhile, sees, and wants to see, the other merely as an enemy to be eliminated, and a contemptible enemy at that since he is incapable of wanting the good or of recognising it' according to their dystopia.

7

Universal vs Unique Values, Multiculturalism vs Monoculturalism

The gruesome, barbaric attack on Israel on 7 October 2023 by Hamas terrorists needs to be condemned by all. Many celebrated the attack, even though it involved the horrific killing of the elderly, the rape of women, parading them naked, and the beheading of children. No state can remain a mute spectator to this. Where were the Wokes, the peaceful and the human rights lobby then? There was silence as deep as the graveyard. Let me congratulate Prime Minister Modi for his courageous stand in of supporting peace and order against terror where rape, loot, and plunder are being normalised. This war is about order versus terror. These people tell us that terror has no religion. Then why is there support for terror groups? Indiscriminate violence and barbarity cannot be part of any peaceful religion. Then there are issues of interpreting values: are values universal or unique?

Values, defined as "desirable, trans-situational goals, varying in importance, that serve as guiding principles in people's lives" play a pivotal role in shaping human behaviour and societal norms. However, the landscape of values is intricate, marked by universal principles, objections to their universality, and the nuanced application of values in different contexts. Universality in values involves shared core principles across diverse cultures, societies, and historical periods. Isaiah Berlin's perspective emphasises that universal values are held by many individuals across various situations, either consciously or expressed in behaviour. Amartya Sen offers an alternative lens, suggesting universality when all people have a reason to believe that a value is valuable.

Universal values form the foundation for moral and ethical judgments, distinguishing right from wrong. Failure to adhere to these values is viewed as a breach of morality and ethics. The existence of universal values sparks debates in moral philosophy and cultural anthropology. The transcendence of cultural, religious, and geographical boundaries characterises these values. Samuel Huntington's influential thesis on the 'Clash of Civilisations' adds a layer to the discourse on universal values. Huntington suggests that cultural and civilisational differences will be the primary sources of conflict in the post-Cold War world. This challenges the assumption of universal values, proposing a world where distinct civilisations have divergent values and interests. He believes that some of the factors contributing to this conflict are that both Christianity (upon which Western civilisation is based) and Islam are missionary religions, seeking conversion of others and are Universal, 'all-or-nothing' religions, in the sense that both sides believe that only their faith is the correct one. These teleological religions represent the goals of existence and purpose in human existence.

More recent factors contributing to a Western-Islamic clash, Huntington wrote, are the Islamic resurgence and demographic explosion in the Islamic world, coupled with the that is, the view that all civilisations should adopt Western values—that infuriate Islamic fundamentalists. All these historical and modern factors combined, Huntington wrote briefly in his *Foreign Affairs* article and in much more detail in his 1996 book, would lead to a bloody clash between the Islamic and Western civilisations. Core state conflicts can arise out of fault line conflicts when core states become involved. Huntington suggests that cultural and civilisational differences will be the primary sources of conflict in the post-Cold War world. This challenges the assumption of universal values, proposing a world where distinct civilisations have divergent values and interests.

Moral relativism opposes the concept of universal moral values, asserting that moral principles are context-dependent. Aesthetic relativism extends beyond aesthetics, challenging the universality of values within different cultural norms. Universal values include justice, which emphasises fairness, impartiality, and equitable resource distribution. It guides ethical judgments and interventions promoting equality. Empathy and kindness, particularly towards those in need, are also universal values. It is essential in designing interventions that enhance social support networks. Additionally, respect for the intrinsic value of all living beings guides behaviours that prioritise environmental care and well-being. Finally, integrity emphasises honesty, truthfulness, and adherence to moral principles and informs interventions fostering trust and reliability in societal interactions.

Individuals and organisations often camouflage parochial values as 'universal' to gain acceptance and popularity. Terrorism, disguised as a 'freedom movement', exemplifies the misuse of universal values for political ends. Woke culture frequently positions itself as a champion of universal values, emphasising principles like equality, justice, and inclusivity. Advocates argue that these values should be universally accepted, yet challenges arise in the selective application and potential clash with cultural relativism. It is hardly surprising to observe Woke culture's impact on freedom of expression, potential polarisation, and the fostering of an 'us vs. them' mentality.

Huntington predicts and describes the great clashes that will occur among civilisations. First, he anticipates a coalition or cooperation between Islamic and Sinic cultures to work against a common enemy, the West. Three issues that separate the West from the rest are identified by Huntington as:

- The West's ability to maintain military superiority through the non-proliferation of emerging powers.
- The promotion of Western political values such as human rights and democracy.
- The restriction of Non-Western immigrants and refugees into Western societies. Non-Western countries see all three aspects as a western attempt to enforce and maintain their status as the cultural hegemon.

Unique values are beliefs and principles specific to particular cultures, communities, or individuals. These values are influenced by history, geography, religion, and tradition. Examples include cultural traditions, religious beliefs, and personal values shaped by individual experiences. Cultural tradition includes specific customs, rituals, and practices that are important within a culture. It may not be shared universally, contributing to cultural diversity. Religious beliefs include teachings and doctrines of various religions guiding moral and ethical conduct and significant differences exist between faiths, influencing diverse values. Personal values: but one should remember the common quote here: "You don't need religion to have morals. If you can't determine right from wrong, then you lack empathy not religion." Individual values are shaped by personal experiences, upbringing, and belonging. Priorities such as family, career, or environmental stewardship are examples. Certain values are unique to specific cultures, religions, and societies, resisting easy implementation in other contexts. Contentious ideas like tolerance for violence or marriage practices showcase the diversity of unique values. Unique values often become instrumental in propaganda dissemination. Groups package their ideas as unique values but strive to connect them with larger universal values to gain mass support.

Conflicts arise when universal values clash with a nation's unique values, such as cultural or religious practices. International organisations and diplomatic negotiations traditionally mediate these conflicts by facilitating discussions for mutually acceptable solutions. However, recent trends suggest a shift in international organisations from platforms for engagement to instruments of power projection and manipulation. In instances like the Hamas-Israel war, international organisations have diverted discussions to the morality of Israel's retaliation towards a terrorist attack. Furthermore, failed experiments with forced multiculturalism in some Western countries highlight the dangers of prioritising unique values at the expense of universal values, challenging the very foundations of cooperation and stability.

8

Woke Chokehold on Debate, Discussion is Growing

The entire visit of Prime Minister Narendra Modi to the United States (US) was a spectacular success despite attempts by the Wokes to undermine it. The *Wall Street Journal* reporter who questioned Prime Minister Modi did not address the genocide of minorities in Pakistan but expressed concern about India. Their false cry and misinformation being spread by the Woke media and a former President are in poor taste, ill-timed, and very irresponsible. While the US system arrests a former President, it is democracy, but when the Indian judiciary legally disqualifies a sitting MP, it is portrayed as a threat to democracy and secularism. What double standards in the application of principles of democracy and secularism. This follows the dictum that for the Wokes the application of principles is based on their ideology are for someone and some purpose and the personal is political. Additionally, they have created the so-called civil society NGOs that set their agenda, like the Open Society.

In India, a country renowned for its diverse landscape and rich tradition of open dialogue, the rise of Woke culture poses a deep concern, casting a shadow over the once-vibrant spaces of debate and discussion. Masked under the banner of promoting social justice and inclusivity, this trend fosters an atmosphere of hostility and exclusion towards differing viewpoints—ironically as it may seem. As Woke culture reshapes the discourse in India, it compels us to reflect upon the future of intellectual freedom and the preservation of diverse thought.

But what exactly is this pervasive phenomenon known as 'Woke culture' or 'Wokeism' that has permeated intellectual spheres locally and globally? The term 'Wokes' refers to individuals hyper-aware of social justice issues, advocating for change predominantly through online activism. However, it is essential to note that Wokes do not necessarily represent the majority opinion or the sentiments of the masses. Instead, they often represent a smaller, vocal faction with a particular agenda. Their amplified voices, aligned with like-minded individuals and groups, create an illusion that their views, values, and moral compass hold absolute truth.

Within the realm of Woke culture, characterised by its creators and followers known as Wokes, an exceptional emphasis is placed on morality and righteousness. This heightened focus on morality brings to mind the insights of philosopher Friedrich Nietzsche, who discussed the concept of herd mentality and its influence on moral judgments. Nietzsche astutely observed that the morality associated with herd mentality asserts, "I am morality itself, and nothing else is morality!" This observation resonates when considering the Wokes' tendency to invoke their own version of morality, vehemently asserting that their moral framework is the sole embodiment of what is right, dismissing alternative perspectives.

Wokeism is marked by an unconditional and one-size-fits-all approach to thinking, often leading to selective uproar and the oversimplification of complex ideas or situations. This mindset disregards the need for context and thorough examination, which can spread misinformation and contribute to societal polarisation. Instead of genuinely addressing the intricacies of a specific issue, the emphasis often lies on 'virtue signalling' or projecting an image of moral righteousness. This focus on appearances rather than on the problem at hand hinders meaningful progress and constructive dialogue. In such a situation, it becomes essential to move beyond superficial gestures and prioritise nuanced understanding and thoughtful analysis to foster a more informed and inclusive society. In addition, Woke culture significantly emphasises group identities, elevating social identity above individual experiences and beliefs. This prioritisation of group identities perpetuates the growth of tribalism and intolerance. A divisive mindset takes hold by categorising individuals solely based on their social identity, eclipsing the acknowledgment of diverse personal experiences and viewpoints. This narrowing of focus creates an environment where intolerance towards differing perspectives becomes increasingly pervasive. As a result, the potential for meaningful dialogue and understanding diminishes, hindering progress towards a more inclusive and harmonious society.

A significant consequence of the rising Woke culture is the stifling of free speech and the diminishing space for intellectual discourse. Despite the claims of equality and diversity, Wokeism shuns the opposing viewpoints as unacceptable or offensive. This is frequently achieved through a 'cancelling' approach to dissenting views and ideas. Individuals or their opinions that do not align with the Woke culture are deemed problematic and individuals find themselves ostracised or silenced, leading to a lack of open dialogue and the exchange of ideas.

Applying Wokeism to the Indian context, such as, using Critical Race Theory in discussions on casteism, illustrates a poor understanding of Indian society. These concepts have been constructed within a colonial framework and weaponised to serve hegemonic narratives, often leading to more problems than solutions. The widespread application of Wokeism in these complex contexts highlights the dangers of unconditional and contextually detached thinking. It exposes how individuals with bitter sentiments exploit resentment to perpetuate a harmful narrative. It is crucial to recognise that these developments undermine both individual and societal values in an endless pursuit of radical liberal ideas.

The many notions that Woke culture promotes indeed have merit in the sense that individuals, groups, and society have genuine grievances. Such concerns and grievances should never be negated or downplayed. However, the approach promoted by Woke culture is counterproductive. Long-standing problems such as casteism and gender inequality require thoughtful and comprehensive solutions rather than quick-fix remedies. The misinformed smear campaigns against those who do not conform with Woke culture's thinking will neither solve any problems nor serve as a substitute for genuine discussions on critical issues, such as gender inequality. Relying on selective content and incomplete information only exacerbates grievances and widens existing societal divides.

Ages before the concepts of free speech and public debate emerged in the West, India had a rich tradition of dialogue and discussion through institutions such as *sabhas* (assemblies) and *samitis* (committees) that provided platforms for debates and discussions encompassing not only political matters but also societal issues and individual differences. India's reputation for diversity has garnered global recognition and admiration. However, the alarming rise of mob mentality observed on platforms like Twitter and other social media demonstrates how this very diversity can become a vulnerability, leading to profound harm inflicted upon society and its institutions. Repairing these divisions often requires extensive time, spanning decades or even centuries while creating or exacerbating differences can occur swiftly, as exemplified by the current political climate to which Woke culture invariably contributes.

The encroachment of Woke culture into academia and media has raised concerns over India's diminishing space for diverse viewpoints and intellectual exchange. Operating under the guise of championing the marginalised and oppressed, Woke culture promotes a predominantly left-leaning narrative that allows little room for alternative perspectives. Universities, which should ideally foster robust ideological debates, often become battlegrounds for intense ideological contestation, with the left maintaining a significant presence. Through buzzwords like 'cultural appropriation', 'microaggression', and the demand for 'safe spaces', Woke culture seeks to validate its moral high ground. However, in practice, it marginalises dissenting voices and stifles meaningful engagement. While the specific subjects and themes may vary over time, the overarching outcome remains unchanged. This reality is apparent in the daily trending hashtags on platforms like Twitter, where rampant bullying and harassment undermine the very social and intellectual space the platform was intended to provide.

Within academia and media, the prevalence of Woke culture has given rise to echo chambers, where individuals primarily seek out and interact with viewpoints that align with their beliefs. This phenomenon has led to the oversimplification of complex issues and a noticeable absence of meaningful engagement with opposing perspectives. Academic freedom is a cornerstone of higher education, allowing scholars to pursue knowledge and ideas without fear of censorship or retaliation. The rise of Wokeness (and cancel culture) undermines this freedom. Cancel culture fosters an environment of ideological conformity, something George Orwell pointed out in his novel, *1984*, wherein specific viewpoints or perspectives are labelled unacceptable and subsequently silenced.

The rise of Woke culture has necessitated that universities to assume a crucial role in restoring balance to public debate. As purveyors of knowledge and intellectual rigor, universities hold the responsibility to counteract the excesses of Woke culture by upholding the principles of open dialogue, critical thinking, and evidence-based reasoning. Universities must actively engage in rigorous research, analysis, and scholarly inquiry, counterbalancing the dogmatic tendencies of Woke culture. By promoting diverse perspectives and fostering an environment of respectful discourse, universities can encourage the exploration of multiple viewpoints and challenge the one-sided narratives often perpetuated by Woke culture.

Furthermore, academia must prioritise disseminating accurate and nuanced information, countering the spread of misinformation prevalent in woke culture. This should also include providing space for the other side to present their viewpoints and ideas. By encouraging evidence-based reasoning and critical analysis, universities should serve as the proverbial lighthouse in the storm of cancel culture and Woke ideology to equip individuals with the tools to critically evaluate ideas, navigate complex issues, and discern fact from fiction. They are also responsible for cultivating intellectual humility, emphasising that knowledge is an ongoing process and that beliefs should remain open to scrutiny and revision. This approach counters the inherent rigidity and self-assuredness often associated with Woke culture, encouraging individuals to self-reflect and consider alternative perspectives. In an era characterised by the unchecked growth of the culture of Wokeness and the pervasive climate of political correctness, public space, particularly the intellectual sphere, have become heavily polluted. The prevailing narrative has devolved into a binary framework where opposing viewpoints are silenced. In this critical juncture, universities and media must rise as beacons of light amidst polarisation, misinformation and misguided opinions. They must reclaim their role as centres of critical debate, open dialogue, and substantive discussions on contentious issues, sorely absent from the broader public discourse.

9

Cancel Culture and Public Space in India

The huge uproar over a film and the politics surrounding its ban in India is extremely unfortunate for the same applies to the content of the National Curriculum Framework. The same textbooks were revised in 2006, yet no protests occurred. Those who represent the hegemonic narrative before 2014 believe they are divinely ordained to write the final word on history, and nothing could follow their final word. Any dissenting opinion or fact is branded a misnomer or trolled endlessly. Through a well-coordinated ecosystem, the hegemonic Left vilifies anyone who disagrees with such curated narratives. This raises the vital issue of freedom of speech and creative expression in the country, highlighting the absence of diversity and a preference for hegemony and exclusivism in intellectual and public space within and outside India. One sees this in the treatment of Karan Kataria at LSE. Had Karan not been a Hindu, would his case have been handled the same way? These are the issues worth debates and discussing.

India's democracy is reaffirmed after the Congress' victory in Karnataka and Electronic Voting Machines are reliable. Yet, the same ecosystem previously claimed that Indian democracy and diversity were in danger. This was being said in India and abroad by supporters like George Soros. However, democracy and diversity are not determined by electoral victories and defeat. Indian democracy is deeply rooted and as old as our civilisation.

The advent of social media has been celebrated as a public good. However, the negative side of social media still needs to be understood through serious research within the academic discourse. Social media is blamed for promoting and sometimes perpetuating cancel culture. However, social media should be understood as a medium rather than the initiator of such ill practices. The cancel culture exemplifies the failure to fully comprehend stands the risks associated with social media.

Cancel culture is loosely defined as a contemporary phenomenon in which individuals or groups seek to publicly ostracise or punish others for their actual or perceived transgressions against certain social norms or values. Individuals or organisations are presumed guilty without due process, leading to loss of employment, reputational damage, psychological distress, and even legal actions. Given the visibility and speed of social media, cancel culture relies on social media campaigns that quickly escalate and become viral, resulting in swift and severe (and sometimes unfair) consequences for the targeted individual or organisation. However, a fascinating aspect about these norms and values that cancel culture promotes is how they change depending on the context and the individuals involved. Simply put, the same rules do not apply to everyone.

Cancel culture is an extreme example of distorting the benefits of social pressure. It is commonly used to dismiss or target anyone with a slightly different opinion. Hate speech is unacceptable, but social reprobation is still a necessary component of free speech. One can freely speak their mind, but one should be aware of the consequences. As the saying goes, "You cannot have your cake and eat it, too." In his recent book, *Cancel This Book: The Progressive Case Against Cancel Culture*, a human rights lawyer and free speech advocate, Dan Kovalik, argues for the necessity of free speech in public spaces. He remarks, "speech that offends but does not interfere with another's right of participation should not be banned or otherwise suppressed. Rather, such speech … should be met with speech; with argument and dialogue, to advance both free speech and hopefully, equality."

A herd mentality traverses cancel culture where any discomfort or disagreement does not prompt self-reflection or fact checking. Instead, it becomes a cue to cancel the person or the idea. The most significant pathology of cancel culture is an ever-changing goalposts where behaviour is condemned regardless of its reasons, simply because someone feels offended. Another pathology of cancel culture emerging is 'selectivity'. Some issues, content, or ideas are acceptable in one setting or when endorsed by like-minded individuals. However, when others raise similar problems, they are condemned as insensitive, ill-informed, or accused of politicising the issue.

Besides negating facts and being selective, cancel culture promotes the mob mentality that ultimately leads to the death of reason, independent thinking, and, most importantly, due process. Some hateful actions or ideas, like Nazism, deserve to be curtailed and banished. However, criticism of Nazism is not based on a convenient alignment of interests but on facts and informed knowledge of its abhorrent Nazi ideas. Moreover, the lack of due process results in many victims being undeservedly besmirched. Cancel culture also causes significant rifts in society where even the dead are not safe, and this culture readily becomes a witch hunt.

In the Indian case, before the film The Kerala Story could reach the theatres, a vicious campaign began that, in a Goebbelsian manner, articulated falsehoods and double standards as truth. Had it been a critique of Hindus, it would have been labelled secular and its release would have been linked with saving democracy in India. However, since the roles was reversed this time, the intolerant fringe refused to accept the reality and the facts and attempted to shoot down the messenger. Such an issue should have been championed by the so-called women's studies centres in universities, which have turned a blind eye since it does not align with their agenda.

The troubling issue with cancel culture is the convenience of labelling that accompanies it. The labels are created and imposed at the lightning speed of social media. These labels cut short the room for context, nuances, or fact-checking. As a result, before the issue or an idea appears in the public domain, the judgments are ready on how to receive them. This is evident in the case of Karan Kataria, whose Hindu identity automatically labelled him as an Islamophobe. Similarly, the appreciation or even acceptance of the film The Kerala Story meant that the individual was considered an Islamophobe. In both cases, labels were imposed, the merits of the situations were sidelined, while evidence for such labelling was never provided. Another sad reality that cancel culture raises is the growing denial and aversion to facts, regardless of how widespread they may be. Despite the numerous real-life instances that The Kerala Story builds upon, there were no attempts at reviewing the incidence of the concern that the film raises. Other notable examples, such as the statements by the former Chief Minister of Kerala, V.S. Achuthanandan, who noted in 2010, "They (the ruling party) want to turn Kerala into a Muslim-majority state in 20 years. They are using money and other inducements to convert people to Islam. They even marry women from outside their community in order to increase the Muslim population," are also conveniently left out of the dominant narratives.

What is concerning about the growing trend of cancel culture is that it prevents certain issues and ideas from reaching the public, even though it may not be convenient. Here emerges another pathology of cancel culture: political correctness, which it seeks to promote and champion. We must ask: what happens when one bows down to the cancel culture and seeks to expose the truth? The answer is, fateful incidents like the 'Rochdale child sex abuse' in Great Manchester, UK. This horrible episode involved abuse and sexual exploitation of underage girls in Great Manchester over several years. What is chilling about this horrific episode is the failure of the system to address the issue because of political correctness, as most of the offenders were Pakistani British. For this reason, the insistence on free speech in public spaces is needed to see uncomfortable facts to address such problems rather than cancelling them because they do not align with one's narratives and agendas.

Finally, we must ask why public spaces are being taken over by these cancel culture supporters in a vibrant democracy like India which will hold the largest elections in the history of mankind next year. The smear campaigns and perverse system of labelling individuals and organisations and conveniently refusing to listen to them have long-term consequences for individual development and society at large. It is important to remember that cancel culture breeds an environment of fear and self-censorship, where individuals are afraid to express themselves for fear of being 'cancelled'. In today's increasingly polarised societies, it is essential to listen to those who are different from us. Allowing them space would foster a harmonious society and lead to a better understanding of one another.

Indian Knowledge Systems (IKS)

10

Higher Education Agenda for New Government

India, the mother of Democracy, has successfully conducted the largest and most extensive elections in history. While the credibility of Indian democracy has been profusely questioned over the last few months, the electoral process has once again demonstrated the robustness of Indian democracy. The triumph of the Bhartiya Janata Party-led National Democratic Alliance government in the 2024 Lok Sabha elections is historic and consequential for various reasons. For the first time since 1962, the incumbent government has secured a third consecutive electoral victory.

Meanwhile, the Congress Party has failed to reach the three-digit mark in Lok Sabha seats for the third consecutive time, despite showing an improved performance compared to the 2019 elections. As is with every election, there were various shocks and surprises. However, as the dust settles on the elections, more impending concerns emerge regarding the future agenda of the new government. What will be and what should be the government agenda for the next five years? The question is easier to pose than to answer it. Let's explore it in the context of higher education.

Streamlining Higher Education

Narrative power sustains political power. In the last decade, little has been done to effect a narrative change, let alone a paradigm shift. It is time academics and intellectuals be involved in the paradigm shift which must be inclusive while celebrating diversity. Uniformity and centralisation may derail the narrative power. The increase in public education investment has not risen from 3.3 per cent to 6 per cent of the Gross Domestic Product (GDP); rather, it has to go to 10 per cent for it is education where narrative power lies.

In 2014, the new government faced significant backlogs and ineffective institutions that hindered economic development and infrastructure. Over the past decade, the government's priority efforts in the education sector were, therefore, focused on rectifying these issues. The remedial measures adopted by the government prolonged the implementation of new policies, as it found itself heavily burdened by the need for extensive corrections across various governance sectors, removal of outdated policies, and the reforms of institutions that no longer served modern educational needs.

A prime example of stagnation in the education sector was the outdated National Education Policy (NEP) of 1986, which had lagged amidst significant global transformations. To address this, the government launched the NEP in 2020, a visionary document designed to tackle various themes and issues across all subjects and education levels. However, its implementation has been hampered by existing bottlenecks and complexity, given that education is a concurrent list subject in the Seventh Schedule of the Indian Constitution. Some institutions have been particularly hesitant or slow to adopt the NEP, due to political reasons and a lack of awareness.

The streamlining efforts initiated by the government in 2014 were decisive in bringing about change. The NEP is unique in its ambition to elevate the education system at all levels, including higher education, by establishing expansive, multidisciplinary institutions. It advocates for teaching higher education in local languages, nurturing multidisciplinary learning, and developing critical and analytical thinking. Other key aspects include granting autonomy to faculty and institutions, overhauling educational methodologies, promoting an optimal learning environment and ensuring merit-based appointments and instituting a National Research Foundation (NRF).

Despite its ambitious and competitive nature, the NEP 2020 also stands out for its strong emphasis on equity and inclusion, ensuring that no individual is prejudiced based on class, caste, gender, or religion. The policy is designed to create an inclusive education system that provides equal opportunities for all, addressing the diverse needs of India's population. By promoting equitable access to quality education, the NEP 2020 aims to bridge existing gaps and foster a more just and inclusive society. The NEP and other regulatory policies are foundational for more significant transformations, and ensuring their speedy and effective implementation should be the government's foremost priority.

Competent and Competitive HEIs

Under the overarching objective of *Viksit Bharat*, the new government must prioritise a comprehensive array of institutional and individual interventions to foster a highly competent and globally competitive higher education sector. Despite India's commendable contributions across various scientific fields, including significant research citations and a world-renowned Information Technology (IT) sector, the current competence of the Indian higher education sector does not align adequately with its global recognition. This discrepancy is particularly evident in India's struggle to attract foreign collaborations and international students to the extent expected, given its inherent capabilities and potential.

However, a discernible shift in themes and discourse within the educational landscape signals a changing attitude towards higher education. This transformation is marked by a departure from traditional metrics focused solely on increasing the number of graduates to a more nuanced emphasis on cultivating a skilled workforce that is outcome-oriented innovative and globally competitive. This paradigm shift underscores the critical importance of interdisciplinary and multidisciplinary approaches in higher education. Initiatives such as the introduction of social sciences courses at prestigious institutions like the Indian Institutes of Technology (IITs) and the integration of technology and coding modules into humanities curricula reflect this evolving perspective.

Encouraging Social Sciences and Humanities

While discussions about the development of higher education often revolve around fields like engineering, biotechnology, science, and technology, it is crucial to recognize that the humanities and social sciences are equally vital components. Unlike the rapid advancements in STEM fields, progress in these areas typically requires long-term investment. With renowned institutions like the IITs and Indian Institutes of Management (IIMs), India holds a significant advantage in these fields. However, the country has faced challenges in competing globally in the humanities and social sciences.

As frequently depicted in international media landscapes, these disciplines are pivotal in shaping our understanding of the world, including its organisation, functioning, and manipulation. Whether it is international relations, sociology, anthropology, mass communication, or political science, India's portrayal and understanding in the global arena depend significantly on these disciplines. Therefore, nurturing individuals who are well-versed in critical thinking and technological aptitude through higher education is imperative for India's trajectory. The new government should prioritise allocating energy and resources to strengthen humanities and social sciences education without compromising the STEM fields. This should involve incremental investment in the education budget to ensure the holistic development of individuals equipped with diverse skills necessary for India's progress and global competitiveness.

The recent electoral cycle in India witnessed unprecedented misinformation and manipulation, primarily through media and social media platforms. For example, a pervasive argument in the news and media suggested that democracy in India had died and that the country had become a 'fascist dictatorship' governed by a few upper castes. Without any evidence, this claim was amplified until it entered public consciousness. Although the elections have proven these assertions untrue, but the damage to the psyche of Indians and India's global image is significant, and the repercussions are visible.

To counteract this, the government must emphasise the development of social sciences, preparing a generation of young Indians who are not sycophants or ideologues but rather reasonable, articulate, and capable individuals. These individuals should be able to defend India's case globally and ensure that the spirit of democracy and the electoral process is respected rather than ridiculed for vile political agendas. Strengthening education in international relations, political science, sociology, and mass communication will be a crucial agenda for the new government. Only narrative power can achieve this. Therefore, this will sustain political power and reflect the reality of leadership.

As the government embarks on its third consecutive term, it has a unique opportunity to effect transformative change within the education sector. Holistic development of all disciplines is necessary, not just the lopsided development of fashionable ones. All stakeholders—government, educators, students, and administrators—must collaborate in synergy to leverage this opportune moment. The continuity advantage of the NDA government, under the leadership of Prime Minister Narendra Modi, should be utilised so that India and Indians equip themselves to compete in the global marketplace of ideas, present our perspectives, and make a compelling case for a *Viksit Bharat*—a developed India.

11

Classical Indian Buddhism and Indian Knowledge Systems

"Since all is empty, all is possible."

– Nagarjuna

Buddhism holds a significant place within India's intellectual and civilisational legacy. It spread to the world from India. Classical Indian Buddhism is a treasure trove of sources in building Bharatiya Gyan Parampara. The *Bharatiya* narrative architecture must reclaim, reimagine, and reconstruct this philosophical tradition. One great philosopher who has fascinated many is Nagarjuna (c. 150-250). Sometimes called the 'second Buddha' in Tibetan and East Asian Mahayana traditions, Nagarjuna was an Indian Buddhist monk and philosopher. He hailed from the present-day Andhra Pradesh. He systematised Mahayana Buddhist philosophy around the central concept of the emptiness (*shunyata*) of all existents (dharmas). He introduced the Madhyamaka or Middle Path philosophy. Moreover, the inclusive and universal nature of Buddhist philosophy underscores and reflects the notions of diversity, dissent, and harmony characterised by Indian civilisation.

Inclusivity and Non-Exclusionary Nature of IKS

Contrary to many caricatures, IKS embodies a spirit of inclusivity that transcends religious boundaries and embraces diverse sources of wisdom. Central to this ethos, is the recognition that knowledge is universal and extends beyond the confines of any particular religious tradition. While Hinduism has made seminal contributions to IKS, including foundational texts such as the Vedas and Upanishads, it is crucial to acknowledge the pluralistic nature of Indian civilisation and the syncretic exchange of ideas that have enriched its intellectual heritage.

Buddhism embodies an inclusive ethos, offering a distinct perspective on reality and the human condition that complements rather than contradicts the Hindu philosophical system. The great philosopher, often referred to as the second Buddha, contributed to the Middle Way philosophy in his text *Mūla-madhyamaka-kārikā* (Fundamental Verses of the Middle Way) from the important tradition of Mahayana Buddhist philosophy.

In the Tao of Physics, Capra highlights out the contemporary relevance of the Classical Indian Buddhist philosophy to nuclear and quantum physics. We must reconstruct the ideas of Nagarjuna. Just take the opening stanza of the text *Mūla-madhyamaka-kārikā*, "Neither from itself, nor another, nor both, nor without cause does anything arise." This encapsulates out the Karmic law of cause and effect, which operates without recourse to a creator, God or any other entity outside this web of mutual interdependence. Every phenomenon arises within the web of causes, making isolated, independent phenomena impossible. The interdependent reality includes all mental processes. Buddhists emphasise that ultimate reality is itself devoid of self-existence. Buddhism embodies the inclusive ethos of IKS.

Buddhist Philosophical Foundations

The philosophical tenets of Buddhism as promoted by the IKS include impermanence (*anitya*) and non-self (*anatman*), which have been subjects of scholarly inquiry and empirical study in India for centuries. Meditation, an integral component of Buddhist traditions, has emerged as a powerful tool to address modern concerns such as stress and high-activity lifestyles. Neuroscientific research has provided evidence that meditation practices like mindfulness induce structural changes in the brain, which are associated with increased emotional regulation, attentional control, and empathy.

The notion that things lack any self-existence is called '*shunyata* (emptiness)'. This is due to two reasons: one, that everything is a flux of momentary instants or '*kshana* (moment)', and two, these moments succeed each other in a perpetual stream. These momentary episodic existences are all mutually caused and are known as '*Pratītya-samutpāda*' (dependent organisation) or co-arising. They do not endure beyond a single moment and are distinct entities. All events, moments, or things are linked and interdependent. The interdependent reality includes all mental processes.

Encouraging Ethics and Morality

As both an academic discipline and a religious practice, Buddhism carries significant societal implications, particularly in fostering ethical principles that promote prosocial behaviour and social cohesion. In the diverse landscape of Indian society, these tenets exemplify inclusive and harmonious cohabitation, which, historically, has been less common in other societies. Individuals influenced by Buddhist concepts such as compassion and interconnectedness tend to exhibit greater altruism and cooperation, even in economic contexts.

Contrary to the assumption that market-oriented policies may promote greed and crony capitalism, the incorporation of Buddhist principles can contribute to the establishment of a robust economic system rooted in trust and long-term incentives for individuals to participate. Research exploring the relationship between adherence to Buddhist moral precepts and subjective well-being has shown positive correlations between ethical conduct and various measures of life satisfaction, psychological flourishing, and resilience to adversity. These findings underscore the enduring relevance of Buddhist ethics in fostering virtuous living and cultivating harmonious societies.

Mindfulness and Mental Well-Being

The study and promotion of Buddhism within the IKS are no longer merely tools for cultural promotion or elements of soft power. While such endeavours may have latent benefits, promoting Buddhist traditions is increasingly viewed as a means of fostering a healthier lifestyle, supported by scientific evidence from clinical psychology and neuroscience. Meta-analytic reviews have consistently demonstrated the effectiveness of mindfulness-based practices such as mindfulness-based stress reduction (MBSR) and mindfulness-based cognitive therapy (MBCT) in alleviating symptoms of anxiety, depression, and chronic pain across diverse populations. These findings shed light on the neural mechanisms of mindfulness practices', showcasing alterations in brain networks associated with attentional control, emotion regulation, and interoceptive awareness.

Thus, in addition to its religious facets, studying Buddhist traditions epitomises the essence of the IKS—the quest to develop knowledge based on *pramāṇa* (evidence). The philosophical tenets of Buddhism that delve into the nature of reality, the concept of endurance, and the path to freedom are paramount requirements for this day and age. The Middle Path of *Nāgārjuna*argues that emptiness makes change and action possible. He points out that existence through essence is untenable because change would be impossible. This is Nagarjuna's death blow to all synthetic unities as they start with separate essences and then seek unity. He advocates for integral unity.

In a world grappling with uncertainty and unrest, the enduring legacy of Buddhism shines as a beacon of hope and enlightenment. Thus, the Buddhist Madhyamaka (Middle way) logic emphasises the context in which truths can be known. It rejects the tyranny of Western hegemonic discourses of exclusivism. Buddhism offers *Dharma* (duty) metaphysics and a *Bharatiya* (Indian) narrative architecture that share common principles, symbols, and techniques, that enrich the Indian Knowledge Systems or the *Bharatiya Gyan Parampara* (Indian Knowledge Tradition).

12

Inclusive and Expansive: A Bharatiya Narrative for Climate Change

The *Panchabhoota Bharatiya* narrative architecture for the ecosystem is holistic, as it views human beings as a part of it in this nature-centric system, where chaos is creative and leads to balance and harmony with the larger cosmos. This contrasts with the hegemonic concept of conquering and destroying nature for the benefit of humans, better known as anthropocentrism. The concept of Devrai, or sacred forests in India, brought sanctity to preserving and protecting biodiversity and Mother Nature. They are the sacred stewards of conservation. This alternative narrative, needs to be constructed as the world faces a huge crisis of reckless development, leading us to calamity.

Bharatiya gyan parampara (wisdom) has taught us to revere the *Panchabhootas* and the Ecosystem. While growing up, we are told by elders to never to play with the *Panchbhoots*, for these natural forces, if disturbed, can engulf humans. Any disturbances of this balance and harmony have had severe natural consequences, where humans have been shown to be helpless against the forces of Nature or the Panchabhootas. Nature is a great leveller.

Since the onset of industrialisation, the climate has been steadily warming. However, the broader challenge lies in the uneven and flawed approach to addressing environmental and climate issues worldwide. The current discourse on climate change originates from the West and is predominantly human-centric, thus often disregarding and even opposing the intrinsic forces of nature and while overlooking indigenous communities. Three key points must be emphasised and understood as the world grapples with increasingly severe and erratic weather events.

Firstly, climate change and environmental protection are not solely governmental or individual concerns but universal imperatives. While it is the responsibility of governments to safeguard the environment from degradation and exploitation, it is equally incumbent upon citizens to contribute to its preservation. In essence, environmental protection is both a top-down and bottom-up process. Many climate initiatives view it solely as a governmental responsibility, holding governments accountable for unmet ecological goals. Undoubtedly, governments bear a significant responsibility, but what about the role of citizens? Enter India, with its millennia of wisdom and a profound understanding of the interplay between humans and nature, characterised by harmony rather than conflict. Indian constitutional thinkers demonstrated foresight by including provisions for environmental protection as far back as 1948 to 1950, long before modern environmental concerns gained widespread recognition in the 1960s and 1970s, notably with Rachel Carson's *Silent Spring*. Even today, governmental approaches in India reflect this deep understanding, evident in the arrangements made with tribal communities and efforts to engage citizens in environmental stewardship. Initiatives such as the Swachh Bharat campaign, the world's largest of its kind, and the integration of environmental awareness into the Indian education system signify steps to elevate awareness of ecological concerns. These actions demonstrate a concerted effort to ensure that the locus of responsibility is not solely limited to the government but that citizens are recognised as equal stakeholders in environmental preservation.

Secondly, environmental discourse must adopt an inclusive approach. Herein lies the significance of India's tradition of *Panchbhoot*. The fundamental constituents of nature are rooted in the principles of *Panchbhoots*—land, water, air, soil, and fire. This perspective places humans not at the centre of the universe, but as an integral part of nature's ecosystem. While the Western viewpoint often seeks to exert control over nature, the Indian perspective rejects human attempts to control nature. In Hinduism, sacred tree groves are revered, while Buddhism includes sacred deer parks. The concept of 'sacred groves' extends beyond specific religious contexts to encompass natural habitats protected on religious grounds. References to sacred groves can be traced back to ancient treatises like *Vrikshayurveda* (The Science of Trees) and literary works such as Kalidasa's *Vikramorvashiyam* (The Hero and the Enchantress). The five elements need to be elaborated upon. There is substantial scientific evidence to show that water has tremendous memory. Just by generating a thought while looking at the water, the molecular structure of the water will change. If one touches it, it will change. So, how one approaches water is very important. Air or '*vayu*', which means not just air as a mixture of nitrogen, oxygen, carbon dioxide and other gases, but as a dimension of movement. Among the five elements, air is the most accessible and relatively the easiest element to gain reasonable mastery over. In Indian culture, the element of fire is personified as *Agni Deva*, a god with two faces who rides on a fiery ram. The two faces represent fire as a life-giver and a life-taker. Without the fire burning within us, there is no life; but if not taken care of, fire can quickly go out of control and consume everything. Akasha is not empty space, nor is it ether, which is the closest translation. It is a subtle dimension of existence. Space is *kala* or non-existence; it is Shiva that which is not and Akasha that which is.

Thirdly, there is a pressing need for more alternative approaches to address climate change issues. This does not presuppose only the Indian approach but encourages local and regional approaches. With its rich tradition and historical context, India embodies an approach that can be encapsulated as 'Global in Scope, Local in Solutions', which is a good starting point. Environmentalists, philosophers, and political leaders in India have advocated for development approaches, prioritising harmony over conflict with nature, reflecting a common thread in their thinking. Integral humanism is one such example that offers insights into understanding environmental issues and developing strategies for their resolution. Cooperation in defence is another theme where Indian traditions can provide valuable lessons to the world. India's initiatives, such as ethanol-blended and hydrogen fuels, exemplify a nuanced approach that eschews simplistic binary positions in favour of locally grounded solutions. Moreover, India is actively embracing and promoting the transition to renewables through global collaborations like the International Solar Alliance and the recently launched Global Biofuel Alliance. In light of the conflicting and competitive climate change models prevalent in global politics, which often divide nations into the Global North vs. Global South or Developed vs Developing countries, India's *Panchabhoota* (five elements) framework emerges as a promising starting point for exploring alternative approaches. It is a cosmos-centric theory where everything in nature and humans has its role in balance and harmony. Any disturbance, such as the anthropocentric approaches where conquering and destroying nature has brought us to where we are today of climate disasters and calamities. Hence, these holistic and nature-centric Indic perspectives underscore a profound connection with nature and the larger cosmos. *Bharatiya gyan parampara* (Indian knowledge tradition) offers a compelling framework for fostering collaboration and collective action on a global scale.

13

Varieties of Democracy (V-Dem) Report 2024: A Political Hatchet Job in the Name of Research

Another year, another report, yet the same story! The V-Dem Institute, based in Sweden, has released its 2024 Democracy Report, once again bringing to the forefront its biases against India and the Global South. The report appears to be a political hatchet job, serving as a mouthpiece for vested interests. With the increasing accessibility of the internet and the public's reliance on digital platforms for news, institutes like V-Dem have found a platform to showcase their supposed virtues without any cost or consequence. Through flashy infographics and diagrams, yet with minimal substance, these reports masquerade as fair and virtuous, akin to high priests from medieval times passing judgment without any legitimate basis or fairness. There is no transparency regarding whose opinions were considered, who these 25 intellectuals are, or the methodology of this purposive, biased, so-called sample or sham opinion of a few.

Non-Academic to the Core

The V-Dem report claims to have 'developed innovative methods for aggregating expert judgments' to produce 'valid and reliable estimates', acknowledging that these estimates are based on 'difficult-to-observe concepts'. Anyone training in research methodology in the social sciences knows that biases and limitations are inherent in concept and practice. Yet, V-Dem seems oblivious to any biases within its operations. Only once does it briefly mention 'potential biases' regarding its report, but swiftly deflects it by attributing such biases to "experts." Then, V-Dem, trying to be the "good guy", claims to address such biases through a 'measurement model'. Thus, a great deal of hyperbole and self-aggrandisement seem enough to overlook academic rigor.

The question of who evaluates V-Dem is also intriguing. According to the methodology outlined on their website, they rely on five 'country experts' in each of five categories, totalling 25 (or so) experts per country, most of whom remain anonymous. These 25 'experts' supposedly serve as better judges of a country's democracy and credentials. Fortunately, India and its Constitution makers wisely opted not to entrust the fate of millions of Indians to a selected few. Instead, they devised a system where people could have a say in the direction of their country through free and fair elections.

Another fundamental aspect of conducting research that V-Dem disregards is revisiting methodologies and reconsidering assumptions. While V-Dem claims to 'continually review' its methodology, it admits that it 'occasionally' adjusts it. The supposedly brilliant methodology employed by organisations like V-Dem regularly faces significant criticism from countries in the Global South, irrespective of their political systems, for their inherent prejudices and ideological narratives that align with the interests of a few like George Soros. Yet, despite years of criticism about its flawed methodology, V-Dem has made no notable endeavour to change its methods. Therefore, the issue at hand transcends concerns about the transparency of the methodology. Instead, it raises significant concerns regarding incompetence and ill-intentions of the so-called report.

Similar to the portrayal often found in Western fiction and oversimplified non-fictional narratives about other parts of the world, the West—mainly comprising the US, Canada, Europe, and Australia—is predictably depicted as a better performer than the rest. However, if Rishi Sunak stops the genocidal calls against Israel and Jews in London streets, the UK would become 'autocratising'. As such, to avoid losing favour with organisations like V-Dem and fear of being labelled as 'authorising', world leaders are getting coz with Woke ideologies.

India in the 2024 Report

India is placed behind countries with questionable and rocky histories of democracy, including Nepal and Kosovo. Labelling a country with 18 per cent of the world's population, which consistently conducts the world's largest elections, as 'one of the worst autocratisers lately' seems quite disproportionate and misguided. Such a characterisation overlooks the complexity and diversity of democratic processes within the country and fails to acknowledge the significant strides made in ensuring democratic participation and representation. What's interesting about the report is that it identifies the process of 'autocratisation' in India beginning in 2008, the same year as India had the 26/11 attacks. Up until then, India had endured two decades of violent, blood-soaked history of terrorism, wherein people died even doing small things such as shopping in the national capital for Diwali. Consequently, when India decided to tackle terrorism and clamp down, particularly over the last decade, it became problematic. The Unlawful Activities (Prevention) Amendment Bill 2019 is cited in the report as one of the reasons for India's poor scores.

Even though terrorism and insurgency-related deaths of civilians and soldiers are at an all-time low in the country, this is deemed irrelevant by V-Dem. It seems that only when India capitulates to Islamic terrorists and insurgents will there be hope for improvement in its rankings. However, this is not an option for India because such rankings do not define India or its people. The democratic process in India is among the most robust in the world, with a history of democratic ideas that is older than many modern-day civilisations.

Politically, some parties may see an opportunity to peddle this dangerous narrative, portraying themselves as doing nothing more than aiding outsiders in spreading misinformation. However, the rankings hold little weight when measured against fundamental academic scrutiny. Disseminating misinformation by V-Dem is critical for countries like India because the impression they create, unfortunately, has a lasting impact. For example, 75 per cent of downloads of V-Dem datasets took place from Europe and North America, which would explain if the behaviour of the European/American investors changed at some point about their investment in India after reading reports that portray the country as intolerant or undemocratic. Such perceptions are misleading and harmful to India's economic prospects. For such reasons, there is an absolute need for action by everyone in India, from students to leaders, to counter such reports. Like many of its counterparts, the V-Dem report must be criticised, condemned, and dismantled, using valid facts and evidence, not only to demonstrate Indian calibre in research but also to dispel the illusion that anything emanating from the West has to be gospel.

Let me reiterate that India is a more durable democracy than many in the West and the rest. No elected leader in a democracy today can match the popularity of the Indian Prime Minister. Narendra Modi's covenant with the world's largest electorate remains unbroken. If authenticity is what leaders lack, even as they seek an eternal mandate, Modi has it in abundance. That adds to the aura of democracy's tallest spokesperson from the oldest and largest democracy. The West must stop preaching and creating false conjectures, prejudices and a colonial hegemonic mindset.

14

Diversity: Jawaharlal Nehru University's (JNU's) Experience of Fighting Stereotypes

UGC's recent draft guidelines on implementing the reservation policy in higher education institutions (HEIs) that proposed the de-reservation of vacancies have got widespread attention, sparking fervent reactions from academia, the public, and the nation. It does not align with Prime Minister Narendra Modi's vision and mission of implementing Bharat Ratna Dr BR Ambedkar's ideas of social, political and economic equity, equality with diversity and inclusion. RSS chief Mohan Bhagwat has supported the continuation of reservations as long as discrimination exists and until the time all forms of equality are achieved for all. Existing regulations clearly state, "a ban on de-reservation of reserved vacancies for SC, ST, and OBC in direct recruitment," according to the Ministry of Education (MoE).

In exceptional circumstances, de-reservation of reserved vacancies can occur if the university provides sufficient justification. In this context, de-reservation involves opening up faculty positions originally designated for specific categories (Schedule Cast (SCs), Scheduled Tribe (STs), Other Backward Classes (OBCs), and Economically Weaker Sections (OBCs) candidates) to applicants from the open category if those positions remain unfilled despite concerted efforts to fill them. This contentious 'draft' has become a focal point of discussion, raising valid concerns about the insensitivity and regressive societal perspectives.

A Regressive Draft

Essentially, the draft highlighted the UGC overstepping its mandate and encroaching into the legislative domain, a prerogative of the Indian Parliament. Worse, it reflected a regressive view of certain individuals, which is unacceptable and condemnable. Thus, the proposed process lacks essential checks and balances, granting the universities with personal prerogatives without consultations with Constitutional bodies, such as, the National Commissions for SCs, STs, OBCs, and other relevant stakeholders, as regulations currently require.

While the draft has been withdrawn, it showcased the persistence of stereotypical thinking despite 75 years of the Indian Republic. More significantly, it draws attention to the stark dissonance on the reservation issue between rhetoric and action, with the former being fashionable and the latter a rare occurrence. As such, a pressing question arises: can we genuinely align words with deeds regarding reservation? The resounding answer is yes. It is not only possible but has been effectively demonstrated by the Prime Minister's vision and mission at JNU marching towards *Viksit Bharat* in 2047—the reality of a developed, equitable, and inclusive Bharat.

The JNU Experience

JNU is a rare exemplar in higher education, translating rhetoric into action. Whether addressing concerns of caste, gender, or other marginalised groups, JNU has emerged as a mainstay of empowerment and upliftment. Our campus proudly leads in creating an inclusive environment, drawing students and faculty from every corner of India. It provides a unique setting, unrivalled even by institutions with massive financial endowments. It epitomises the diverse tapestry of Bharat, where individuals are evaluated not based on caste, creed, colour, religion, or appearance but on their character.

Under the current administration, there is a steadfast commitment to the belief that Ambedkar's seminal work, *Annihilation of Caste*, is not merely a social and political treatise but a fundamental objective that our society must ardently pursue. The present ethos of JNU serves as a living testament to Ambedkar's vision of eradicating casteism. We have opened the windows to allow fresh air to enter.

In its 54-year legacy, JNU proudly asserts that no posts have been de-reserved'. Today, faculty recruitment in the reserved category is at its highest point in -university's history. A meticulous breakdown of recruitment interviews conducted by the current administration over 19 months reveals our commitment to diversity. Individuals from reserved categories constituted an impressive 69 per cent, a commitment reflected in the subsequent recruitment pool. This is why we can say that we have fought the stereotypes and done all this publicly and transparently, with evidence available on both social media platforms and the official JNU website.* Furthermore, JNU has taken noteworthy strides towards breaking gender barriers. A significant milestone is the appointment of the university's first female Vice-Chancellor, which still surprises many. Adding to this milestone, the current administration at JNU stands out as the first to comprise 26 per cent of women in key administrative roles, including chairpersons, deans, and crucial offices such as the Dean of Students and Chief Vigilance Officer. While these advancements may seem intuitive to the younger generation, they were neither arbitrary nor easily achieved. The journey involved considerable resistance and challenges, particularly when addressing entrenched patriarchal and casteist mindsets.

Challenges Remain

The university's initiatives underscore our continuous efforts to forge an inclusive and equitable academic environment, aligning with the imperative progress envisioned by Ambedkar. However, we acknowledge that we are not immune to faults or challenges. Acknowledging such historical lapses and recognising our responsibility to rectify these errors, we reflect on our shortcomings.

Undoubtedly, the journey to tackle patriarchal and casteist mindsets has been met with resistance and challenges. Several centres at JNU lacked even a single faculty member from reserved categories and attempts to address this imbalance faced fierce opposition. Lingering systemic problems

* https://x.com/JNU_official_50/status/1706499491870957979?s=20

have perpetuated these stereotypical mindsets. The current administration is committed to rectifying these historical errors.

Diverse and Inclusive *Amrit Kaal* (Golden Age)

In conclusion, the JNU experience is a compelling illustration that the reservation policy can be implemented efficiently and carefully. Such efforts are integral in inspiring the next generation poised to enter the workforce during the transformative decades, referred to by Prime Minister Modi as *Amrit Kaal* and a *Viksit Bharat* (Developed India) 2047, which is both diverse and inclusive. Our commitment to diversity, evident in our recruitment practices, highlights that fostering a diverse workforce sustains growth and enhances it, reinforcing the adage that diversity is our strength.

Driven not by a desire for superficial changes, accolades or brownie points, we have pursued a firm conviction that institutions and systems fostering casteist ideas must be dismantled, annihilated, and replaced with ideas of diversity and inclusivity. Respecting notions of free thinking and respect for rules, JNU operates within the framework of the Indian Constitution and government regulations. And we feel 'proud' of "implementing the Constitutional guarantees under the Reservation policy as stipulated by MoE." For us at JNU, diversity and inclusivity are not mere catchphrases but core values that define our administration—a commitment to walk the talk.

15

Viksit Bharat@2047: A Clarion Call for Institutes and Students

Last week marked a pivotal moment as Prime Minister Narendra Modi inaugurated a groundbreaking initiative titled '*Viksit Bharat*@2047: Voice of Youth'. This initiative sounded a resounding call to action for Higher Education Institutions (HEIs) and students, providing the youth with a platform to contribute their ideas to the vision of *Viksit Bharat*@2047.

This initiative stands out as the most thrilling and ambitious among all the endeavours in recent decades. The palpable excitement, keen interest, and burgeoning hopes since its launch in less than ten days ago attest to its significance. This is indeed an excellent example of participatory democratic development by involving all the stakeholders. One might enquire about the reasons fuelling this fervour; and the answer lies in several compelling factors.

However, three stand out and demand our utmost attention: First, amid the multifaceted transformations that India, as a nation and a civilisation, is currently undergoing on both local and global fronts, this is the time, the right time (*Yahi Samay hai, Sahi Samay hai*) for such an initiative. Deliberately acknowledging the profound significance of *Amrit Kaal*, the initiative resonates with a compelling sense of urgency and opportunity.

Prime Minister Modi underscored that India now stands where the world observes it with awe and scrutiny as it ascends the ladder of achievements and approaches its independence centenary. This reality adds a layer of responsibility to every citizen, particularly the youth. The explicit encouragement to the youth to actively engage in the *Viksit Bharat* initiative and share their suggestions through the Ideas Portal reflects a deep commitment to inclusivity and incorporating diverse perspectives.

As the Prime Minister rightly emphasised, the vision for *Viksit Bharat* should be a collective effort shaped by every citizen. The success of this initiative hinges on the combined endeavours of all, aptly encapsulated by the mantra, *sabka prayas* (everyone's efforts). Second, this vision is not just a superficial aspiration, as we have seen with numerous plans since India's independence.

It is a meticulously crafted strategy with precise details and modalities that are genuinely actionable, significantly increasing the likelihood of its promises turning into successful outcomes. How can one discern this? Consider the stakeholders involved; it is not a random assortment, like students or teachers, as seen in many past government policies. Instead, the initiative identifies four key stakeholders: administration, academic institutions, teachers, and students.

While the onus rightfully rests on the shoulders of the youth, the recognition of administration and academic institutions as stakeholders signifies the government's understanding. It acknowledges that to bring about a substantial difference in the conduct of students and teachers, fostering innovation and excellence requires mechanisms, processes, and, most importantly, a platform.

This might appear as a simple or intuitive observation to some, but a closer examination of higher education policies and legislation reveals how rare such comprehensiveness in planning has been. Another testament to the excellence of this initiative is the launch's adherence to Standard Operating Procedures prepared for universities, colleges, and students.

This ensures that it is not all rhetoric and platitudes but a call to action. Universities and university-level institutions are designated as anchors, serving as the focal point for the government. They must appoint a dedicated team to promote, organise, disseminate information, and mobilize students for this initiative.

The government outlines four clear interventions: They are firstly, raising awareness through workshops, organising fests involving debates and events, and leveraging existing alumni networks and networked engagement through email groups for swift dissemination. Secondly, developing the requisite infrastructure through dedicated feedback loops in libraries and labs, establishing '*Viksit Bharat* Ideation Centres', and allocating specific slots for students to submit feedback. Thirdly, ensuring holistic participation through wide circulation of forms, recognition of student clubs, including National Cadet Corps and National Service Scheme, and certification. Lastly, tracking progress through daily reports and implementing monitoring and accountability measures. This comprehensive approach sets *Viksit Bharat*@2047 apart, promising tangible and impactful results.

The initiative underscores a crucial yet underemphasized facet—elevating higher educational institutions to unprecedented prominence and ambition. Throughout the post-Independence era, successive governments have endeavoured to introduce structures, regulations, and initiatives within the higher education sector.

However, the limelight has consistently eluded higher education, overshadowed by the pressing concerns of primary and secondary education. While the dearth of attention on primary education may explain this discrepancy, it has persisted for decades without serious rectification.

This oversight led external observers to infer that higher education did not hold a prime position on India's list of priorities. Enter the Modi government, and a paradigm shift in perspective occurs. This administration not only comprehends but boldly asserts that higher education is a challenging yet integral cornerstone of the country's development as a global juggernaut of ideas, innovation, and strength.

Whether it is the establishment of AIIMS facilities nationwide, representing the apex of medical education, or the proliferation of IITs (engineering) and IIMs (management), the government's impetus and vision are crystal clear—higher education is paramount for India's growth as it aspires to ascend to the mantle of a world leader. To conclude, the launch of *Viksit Bharat*@2047 marks a transformative initiative, bringing students and higher learning to the forefront of India's developmental landscape.

With an explicit call to action for higher education institutions (HEIs) and students, this strategic and actionable plan resonates with urgency and opportunity, symbolised by the acknowledgement of *Amrit Kaal*. The comprehensive approach, involving critical stakeholders like administration, academic institutions, teachers, and students, demonstrates a profound commitment to inclusivity and innovation, positioning higher education as a pivotal driver for India's ascent to global leadership.

The Prime Minister has taken us from rule-takers to be rule-shapers, and in 2047, India will move from rule-shapers to rule-makers.

16

JNU will Seek the World: Not its Validation

The goal of becoming a *Vishvaguru* (Global Teacher) in the knowledge society requires transformational reforms in education. The National Education Policy (NEP) 2020, is indeed a unique framework, for it brings in continuity with change, and merges specialisation with a holistic approach. The stress on interdisciplinary and multidisciplinary aspects of knowledge introduces a balance between science, technology, social sciences, humanities, and languages; between the local and the regional, the national and the international, as well as the universal.

The State's role in education is very important, for it is public education that bridges the gap between social, economic, and regional disparities. Private players can never replace the state, as the autonomy of educational institutions is guaranteed by democracies such as India. The weighty yet indispensable responsibility of fostering education and driving innovation is intricately tied to the architecture of our education system. Within this framework, the role of higher education institutions, particularly exemplified by institutions such as JNU, assumes an outsized and pivotal significance. This calls for a higher investment in education by the state, to more than 10 per cent of the GDP.

The role ascribed to institutions of higher learning, including JNU, is to facilitate education, foster innovation, and contribute to the construction of a society characterised by openness, diversity, compassion, self-reliance, self-dignity, and high-calibre competitiveness. Since its inception, JNU has been a vital chapter in India's narrative of higher education. It has functioned as a nurturing crucible for emerging leaders across diverse domains and sectors, from politics to bureaucracy to the armed forces. It has also produced a Nobel Prize winner. Moreover, JNU has championed inclusive, democratic, and creative spaces for discourse, deliberation and discussion, significantly influencing the trajectory of public debates.

While we rightfully take pride in many aspects of JNU, its history, and the institution itself, some challenges demand our attention. The first challenge confronting higher education institutions in India, including JNU, revolves around enhancing their outcomes and outputs. Subsequent challenges, though relevant, complement or augment this central concern. The primary objective at JNU is to extend its impact by assuming a heightened social responsibility—cultivating a workforce that is not only characterised by parity, equity, diversity, and enhanced competitiveness but also one that wields the agency to influence and guide the global future. JNU nurtures a workforce that not only conforms to prevailing global paradigms but also possesses the capacity to shape and lead them. Failing to fulfil this pivotal mission would render JNU's identity as a university and higher education institution incomplete.

The second significant challenge is extending our outreach to marginalised and underrepresented segments of society. JNU has steadfastly positioned itself as an institution that fosters an environment conducive to the progress of women and marginalised groups. In doing this, JNU has not only propagated and extended the concept of *Nari Shakti* (Woman Power, women-led development) but has also served as an embodiment of it. In a remarkable stride, the institution has witnessed appointments of women as chairpersons and deans over the past one-and-half years as well as an increase in the number of women students during the period—a historical precedent that resonates with its commitment to equity and women's empowerment.

The third challenge revolves around infrastructural limitations. Financing remains an enduring struggle for higher education institutions worldwide, presenting fluctuations in resource availability. Although JNU faces fiscal constraints, it has adroitly harnessed technology and alternative sources of revenue to mitigate a range of deficiencies. Pioneering the landscape, JNU is set to become India's first higher education institution with a fully operational 5G-enabled campus, exploring private-public collaboration in infrastructure development. This transformative step underscores our resolve to recalibrate ourselves and bolster competitiveness and efficiency. Such adaptations equip us to effectively address contemporary issues and anticipate the challenges of tomorrow enabling us to yield tangible outcomes.

The fourth imperative is to link tradition with modernity, excellence with empathy, equality with equity and inclusion with integrity and innovation. This transition necessitates a concentrated emphasis on fostering and advancing Indian knowledge systems. The establishment up of Vidyaranya Institute of Knowledge and Advance Studies (VIKAS) is a step in this direction. This includes various aspects, including the promotion of Indian languages. JNU envisions a School of Indian Languages, Culture and Civilisation to foster a better understanding of each other. Under this initiative, a Centre for Tamil Language Studies has been established at JNU, and this will be followed by centres for Assamese, Odia, Kannada, and Marathi languages. While JNU is not the only entity engaged in this endeavour, it aims to assume a leadership role in actualising the visionary NEP 2020.

The challenges elucidated thus far are indeed formidable, but they are not insurmountable. Nonetheless, amidst these considerations, there is also a newfound sense of optimism. We find ourselves fortunate to have access to the guidelines outlined in NEP 2020, which furnish us with a robust blueprint. What is remarkable about NEP 2020 is that it straddles the delicate balance between a structured framework on one hand and the flexibility to effect adaptive changes on the other. The 15 schools, 10 special centres, and our 140 affiliated defence, research, travel, and tourism institutes are implementing many features of NEP 2020.

The biggest challenge is to include the multiple intellectual narratives in India, without excluding anyone. We aim to cultivate a proficiency that attracts the world to us rather than us seeking validation from the world. Looking ahead, our strategy encompasses leveraging the prowess of our alumni network and building upon our notable achievements. Concurrently, we are committed to forging new avenues, exemplified by our emphasis on Indian knowledge systems.

Our Indic civilisation state is a feminist and a nature-centric. We celebrate the Six Ds in JNU—democracy, difference, debate, dialogue, dissent and development. These values are integral to our identity. We have students and faculty from all parts of the country working for the nation's progress in peace and harmony.

Our mission at JNU involves promoting equity alongside equality, intertwining tradition with modernity, seamlessly transitioning between continuity and change, harmonising the universal with the regional, and bridging the gap between theory and practice. Critics might argue that pursuing such an ambitious agenda is rife with inherent contradictions. Yet, in light of India's current aspirations and trajectory, these ambitions are plausible and desirable. Indeed, time will substantiate the veracity of these goals. For such reasons, our goal is clear: We wish to become an integral contributor to India's success story as the country approaches its Independence centenary through innovation, inclusion, diversity, respect, and responsibility.

17

Challenges to Higher Education in Amrit Kaal

The motto of 'Excellence with Empathy, Equality with Equity and Inclusion with Integrity and Innovation' is even more relevant today. The relevance being the spate of suicides by promising young men and women, especially from the marginalized groups—this is extremely distressing to say the least. HEIs must address this issue urgently for there seems to be a lack of empathy, equality and inclusion. It is crucial for all stakeholders to foster a sense of belonging. We need to learn from each other, especially the best practices in empathy, equality and inclusion. These academic spaces need to be created and rigorously maintained.

The goal of becoming a *Vishvaguru*, a leader in the knowledge society requires transformational reforms in education. The NEP 2020 is indeed a unique framework, for it brings in continuity with change, universal with the regional and holism with specialisation. The stress is on interdisciplinary and multi-disciplinary aspects of knowledge, striking a balance between science, technology, social sciences, humanities, and languages. A touch of the local, regional with the national and international as well as the universal.

The State's role in education is crucial, for it is public education that bridges the gap of social, economic, and regional disparities. Private players can never replace the State, as the autonomy of educational institutions is guaranteed by a democratic state like India. Undertaking the weighty yet indispensable responsibility of embracing the endeavour of learning, fostering education, and driving innovation are intricately tied to the architecture of our education system. Within this framework, the role of higher education institutions, particularly exemplified by institutions like JNU, assumes an outsized and pivotal significance. This calls for a higher investment in education by the State to more than 10 per cent of the GDP. Political power without narrative power is like a directionless ship. Science and technology are mere instruments, and a narrative architecture built and nurtured by political power with economic and social power, will enhance the longevity of any political regime.

NEP 2020 is a visionary document that has provided higher education institutions (HEIs) the opportunity to be flexible, experiment and become more inclusive. Once a student is able to gain admission into the top HEIs the feeling of belonging need to be created by the faculty and the seniors, isolation and competition need to be replaced by empathy, learning and mindfulness. Instead of declaring a student a failure in a format of examination, should not be the last word on their abilities. The greatest mathematician, Srinivasa Ramanujan failed to clear his higher secondary exams. It is not only an issue of mental illness, but the environment that contributes to it. HEIs must give that ray of hope to all students. HEIs need work together to resolve these issues and create unalienating spaces.

The role ascribed to institutions of higher learning, including JNU, is to facilitate education, foster innovation, and contribute to the construction of a society characterised by openness, diversity, compassion, self-reliance, self-dignity, and high-calibre competitiveness. From its inception, JNU has been a vital chapter in India's narrative of higher education. It has functioned as a nurturing crucible for emerging leaders across diverse domains and sectors, ranging from the political sphere to the realms of bureaucracy, the armed forces and two Noble Prize winners. Moreover, JNU has fervently championed inclusive, democratic and creative spaces for discourse, deliberation and discussion significantly influencing the trajectory of public debates.

While we rightfully take pride in many aspects of JNU, its history, and the institution itself, some challenges demand our attention. The first challenge confronting higher education institutions in India, including JNU, revolves around enhancing their outcomes and outputs. Subsequent challenges, though relevant, complement or augment this central concern. The primary objective at JNU is to extend its impact by assuming a heightened social responsibility—cultivating a workforce that is not only characterised by parity, equity, diversity, and enhanced competitiveness but also wields the agency to influence and guide the global trajectory. JNU's pivotal role lies in nurturing a workforce that not only conforms to prevailing global paradigms but also possesses the capacity to shape and lead them. This commitment to proactive influence and guidance represents an imperative. Failing to fulfil this pivotal mission would render JNU's identity as a university and higher education institution incomplete. How to incorporate Industry -University cooperation for skill enhancement.

The second significant challenge pertains to extending outreach to marginalized and underrepresented segments of society. JNU has steadfastly positioned itself as an institution fostering an environment conducive to the progress of women and marginalised groups. In doing this, JNU has not only propagated and extended the concept of *Nari Shakti* but has also served as a living embodiment of it. In a remarkable stride, the institution has witnessed the appointments of women as chairpersons and Deans over the past one and a half years—a historical precedent that resonates with its commitment to equity and women's advancement and empowerment. With an increase in the number of girl students and women faculty in the last year and half.

The third challenge revolves around infrastructural limitations. Financing remains an enduring struggle for higher education institutions worldwide, presenting fluctuations in resource availability. JNU faces fiscal constraints, yet it has adroitly harnessed technology and alternative sources of revenue to mitigate a range of deficiencies. Pioneering the landscape, JNU is set to become India's first higher education institution with a fully operational 5G-enabled campus and exploring the private-public collaboration in infrastructure development. This transformative step underscores our resolve to recalibrate ourselves, bolstering competitiveness and efficiency. Such adaptations equip us to effectively address contemporary issues and anticipate the challenges of tomorrow, yielding tangible outcomes.

The fourth imperative is to link tradition with modernity, excellence with empathy, equality with equity and inclusion with integrity and innovation. This transition necessitates a concentrated emphasis on fostering and advancing Indian Knowledge Systems. The setting up of VIKAS is a step in this direction. This includes various aspects, such as the promotion of Indian languages. JNU envisions a 'School of Indian Languages, Culture, and Civilisation' to foster better understanding of each other. Under this initiative, a Centre for Tamil Language Studies has been established in JNU which is poised to be joined by the Assamese, Odia, Kannada, and Marathi languages. While JNU is not the only entity engaged in this endeavour, it aims to assume a leadership role in actualising the visionary NEP 2020.

The biggest challenge lies in embracing multiple narratives within the Indian intellectual horizons without excluding anyone. We aim to cultivate a proficiency that attracts the world to us rather than us seeking validation from the world. Looking ahead, our strategy encompasses leveraging the prowess of our alumni network and building upon our notable achievements. Concurrently, we are committed to forging novel avenues of contribution, exemplified by our emphasis on Indian Knowledge Systems. The Indic Civilisation is a feminist and a nature-centric one. We celebrate the Six Ds in JNU: Democracy, Difference, Debate, Dialogue, Dissent and Development, which are integral to our values. We have students and faculty from all parts of the country working for the nation's progress in peace and harmony.

18

Transform Higher Education by Seizing the Artificial Intelligence (AI) Moment

NEP 2020 has envisioned a holistic, multidisciplinary, and interdisciplinary approach to lifelong education. Change and continuity have been a major thrusts and the introduction of a scientific temper, along with the implementation of latest implementation of technological tools for teaching and research is very important. One such tool is Artificial Intelligence, which brings in new opportunities as well as challenges.

AI is the talk of the town in nearly every discussion across almost every domain. While the transformative potential of AI has been recognised for some time, its widespread applications (such as ChatGPT or Co-Pilot) and evident benefits have now made it a powerful and disruptive force across various industries. Regardless of the industry, AI is becoming essential in shaping the future. Higher education is one sector that stands to gain the most from AI's revolutionary potential. Integrating AI into higher education presents many opportunities to revolutionise the learning experience, advance research and innovation, and address longstanding challenges in the educational landscape.

However, this journey is not without its complexities, and it demands a thoughtful and responsible approach to unlock the full potential of AI while navigating the inherent challenges. The impact of AI in higher education is multifaceted and far-reaching. As an adaptive learning tool, AI has the potential to personalise education, accommodating the diverse needs and learning styles of students. In a classroom setting, where students struggle to obtain the individual attention from the teachers due to the low student-teacher ratios, AI-driven systems can provide personalised instruction, identify strengths and weaknesses, and offer targeted support for better learning outcomes. This customised approach empowers students to progress at their own pace, fostering a deeper understanding and engagement with the subject matter. Moreover, the significance of AI in promoting women's higher education cannot be understated. Historically, cultural barriers, gender norms, and limited access to educational opportunities have impeded women's access to higher education. However, AI-driven language learning tools can break down language barriers and empower women to pursue higher education, irrespective of their linguistic backgrounds. By offering personalised and adaptive learning experiences, AI can support women in acquiring the necessary skills and knowledge to advance their careers and achieve their academic aspirations. This is beneficial for regions with limited access to educational infrastructure. AI-driven tools can bridge the digital divide, offering equitable access to quality education.

The power of AI in research and innovation within higher education is equally profound. Gathering and analysing vast amounts of data enable researchers to make evidence-based decisions, facilitating breakthroughs across various disciplines. AI-driven tools can analyse complex datasets, identify patterns, and offer insights that humans may not easily discern. This data-driven approach fosters a deeper understanding of regional challenges and opportunities, promoting informed decision-making and societal advancement.

Besides the educational benefits, AI-driven tools have much to offer regarding the administration and bureaucracy associated with higher education. Administrative tasks, such as attendance tracking and record-keeping, can be automated using biometric authentication and AI-powered systems. This reduces the administrative burden and promotes transparency and accountability within the educational ecosystem. Institutions can focus more on core educational goals and provide quality learning experiences without exhausting resources and energy on repetitive tasks. Moreover, the documentation required for admissions or transfers could be significantly simplified, alleviating the current burden of complexity associated with these procedures.

Yet, the integration of artificial intelligence into higher education presents several challenges. Ethical concerns and data privacy issues arise from the collection and processing of vast amounts of student data. Establishing robust data protection and privacy policies to safeguard sensitive information and ensure transparent communication with students regarding data usage is imperative. Ethical guidelines must be in place to prevent the misuse of AI-derived insights and data for commercial or discriminatory purposes.

Another challenge lies in the implementation of AI, particularly in regions with limited access to educational infrastructure. Bridging the digital divide demands investment in resources, reliable internet connectivity, and access to digital devices to ensure equitable access to AI-driven educational tools. Comprehensive teacher training programs are essential to equip educators with the necessary skills to maximise AI's potential effectively. Before bringing AI to students, the faculty and the pedagogy need to be updated with the transformative nature of AI. Furthermore, AI education in universities should include learning the ethics of using and employing the technology. AI educators must adhere to ethical standards and data privacy protocols to promote the fair use of technology in the education sector.

In the face of such veritable challenges, a balanced approach is essential for integrating AI into education. While AI can enhance the learning experience, it should complement rather than replace the human element of teaching and mentorship. Effective education entails a symbiotic relationship between AI-driven tools and human intelligence, where educators play a central role in guiding and supporting students' academic journeys. A critical mention must be made of the NEP 2020, which recognises the unfolding significance of AI and its role in shaping the future of education. The policy views AI as a powerful tool to address various challenges and achieve sustainable development goals, including promoting women's higher education. The proactive pursuit of the objectives outlined in the NEP 2020, combined with broader governmental efforts to promote scientific innovation and learning, would yield tangible outcomes that would benefit the country and society in the long term.

The effective implementation of AI in higher education demands collaborative efforts among policymakers, educators, and AI developers. The government must prioritise investment in AI research and infrastructure to foster innovation and ensure equitable access to AI-driven educational tools. Unlike other fields, AI in education would ensure improvements in AI itself as more young minds engage with the technology, making it more efficient, helpful, and safer. To implement AI effectively, educational institutions must embrace a culture of adaptability and provide comprehensive training to faculty members to maximise AI's potential effectively.

Integrating AI in higher education offers a transformative opportunity to revolutionise learning, research, and administrative processes. By leveraging AI responsibly, higher education institutions can unlock their full potential and create a more inclusive and innovative educational environment. The journey toward AI-driven higher education requires collaborative efforts among policymakers, educators, and AI developers to address challenges and seize opportunities. By embracing AI thoughtfully, India can lead the way in shaping a future where AI is a powerful catalyst for advancing higher education, fostering a generation of skilled and empowered individuals ready to take on the challenges of a rapidly evolving world. Essentially, India cannot afford to be complacent as the AI revolution unfolds in education. India must seize this opportune moment with AI, as failing to do so would leave future generations constantly playing catch-up.

19

National Council of Educational Research and Training (NCERT) Deletions: There is No Conspiracy

Recently, alarmist news was circulated that key concepts and segments, notably the theory of evolution and the periodic table, have been dropped from science textbooks by the NCERT. The usual suspects took to social media to declare the death of secularism and scientific temper in India. The story received widespread global attention, including from Al-Jazeera, Deutsche Welle, and the noted scientific journal *Nature*.

What was particularly concerning in this case, was the circulation of unverified information on social media, which was further amplified by mainstream media. From one news outlet to another, the story expanded, sowing disinformation and confusion. This not only had an adverse impact on the reputation of the NCERT but also created scepticism about the country's education system. The government had already been working to dispel the negative image of the country's education system. No scientific theory is absolute; it can be contested. The latest debates that have questioned Darwin's theory of evolution need to also be a included in the curriculum.

The updating of textbooks is a regular process carried out by the NCERT, but one needs to understand that these changes are not random. They are undertaken in specific contexts. First, some changes were made to reflect changing realities—these include the incorporation of content related to information technology and computers. Second, the textbooks are revised in accordance with the reforms in the country's educational system. In this case, the landmark National Education Policy (NEP) 2020 is the guiding principle;—"it emphasises reducing the content load and providing opportunities for experiential learning with a creative mindset."

The current process of rationalisation is motivated by another critical factor: The effects of the pandemic, on the educational system. There was a colossal loss of teaching time during the pandemic which, in turn, led to a loss of learning and increased the load on the students. This was also a concern expressed by the Parliamentary Standing Committee on Education. Therefore, the process of rationalisation was initiated to facilitate the 'speedy recovery in the learning continuum and compensate for the time lost by students'.

The NCERT was tasked with the rationalisation of textbooks across all classes and subjects. The process accounted for five broad criteria: Overlaps with similar content in other subjects within the same class; similar content in a lower or higher class; the level of difficulty; easily available content that does not require much assistance from teachers and can be undertaken through self or peer-learning; and irrelevant content in the present context.

The controversy caused by confusion and misinformation is self-evident. Yet, what's surprising is the sheer absence of follow-up by the critics after the NCERT's clarification. Three observations need to be made in this respect. First, there is a need to gain perspective and separate facts from fiction. The periodic table has 'not been removed from school education curriculum' but has instead been reassigned to Unit 3 in the Class 11 textbook. Darwin's theory of evolution is covered in 'great detail' in chapter six of the Class 12 textbook. The missing reference to Maulana Azad from the Class 11 Political Science textbook (Indian Constitution at Work) is not a part of the current process of rationalisation. The reference was dropped from 2014-15 onwards—and that was finalised for printing in October 2013. Though the reference to Azad was not a part of the current rationalisation process, it ended up being linked with the larger controversy. Many leaders have not been mentioned in textbooks, even earlier.

The major chunk of confusion is caused by the deletion of some items that the critics argued were not included in the notification of the rationalisation. This has nothing to do with some conspiracy but is representative of the regular process of reprinting, where minor deletions are not notified to avoid unnecessary confusion. Scrutiny should be lauded as long as it is rooted in hard facts and evidence. Selective reading and mischaracterisation do not breed transparency or accountability instead, they undermine them.

Second, the discussions have missed another important point—these textbooks are for this year alone. Besides the larger synchronisation practice of textbooks to make them align with the NEP 2020, the textbooks are supposed to be revised regularly by the Textbook Development Committee (constituted in 2005). This committee is mandated to develop the syllabus in line with the 2005 National Curriculum Framework (NCF). Each proposed change is first sent to the Textbook Committee, which is tasked with analysing and recommending them. Moreover, these are not radical transformations since reprinting textbooks to take care of the suggestions of stakeholders is a process that takes place every year.

Third, these decisions were taken by the expert panel. The rationalisation of textbooks is a need-based exercise to reduce content load due to of the toll taken on the mental health of students during the pandemic. The NCERT arrived at these decisions after consulting 'in-house' domain experts, as well as 25 external specialists.

Changes and revisions in textbooks, along with ensuing controversies, are nothing new. In 1978-79, a controversy over revising the contents of history books dominated the political landscape during the short tenure of Prime Minister Morarji Desai. In 2006, during the UPA rule, a chapter on Sikhism had to be changed because of a significant controversy. Another controversial incident occurred in 2012, when the Shahi Imam of the Fatehpuri Mosque in Delhi, Mohammed Mukarram Ahmed, demanded the removal of two mediaeval paintings from history textbooks arguing that their inclusion violated Sharia law.

However, the speed with which the controversy spread, despite India today being better placed to cross-check facts than before, is concerning. Context and facts must be accounted for before any discussion is initiated. Learning about the menace of disinformation is an education in itself. The NCERT controversy shows how easy it is to spread misinformation, but more importantly, how necessary it is to counter misinformation.

20

The National Council of Educational Research and Training (NCERT) Textbook debate is Unnecessary

The recent debate on changes in the (NCERT) history textbooks reminded me of a comment by Russian novelist Leo Tolstoy: "The factors which determine the life of mankind are various; historians select from them only some single aspect, say the political and economic, and represent it as primary, as the efficient cause of social change."

As a social scientist and an administrator, I am dismayed to read in some sections of the media allegations that the corrections and improvements made in the NCERT history textbooks are deliberate distortions or rewriting of our history, that today's historians are less competent, and that they are erasing parts of our history under the influence of a particular ideology.

Such a charge is laughable and betrays a sense of entitlement that only one set of historians from a specific era had the sovereign and absolute knowledge to determine what should be taught about India's civilisational past in our schools.

While the importance of the autonomy of academic and intellectual activities in writing school textbooks, especially for central organisations such as NCERT, can never be overemphasised, the recent kerfuffle on how institutional autonomy has been undermined by the current government and how academic freedom is under stress is a pointless and one-sided exercise.

Nobody has told me what to teach in the last nine years or how to frame my questions on a topic. Turning to the history textbooks prepared by the NCERT, there is a growing demand to improve and correct their content. School textbooks should be revised or rewritten every ten years to incorporate discoveries and new knowledge. This will benefit learners, broaden their horizons, empower them to think independently about our past, political and social systems and understand plans for the future.

The current NCERT social sciences textbooks were prepared in 2006, and as media reports suggest, NCERT has rationalised Class 12 history books, correcting mistakes and errors, rather than rewriting them. However, there is an urgent need for a thorough revision of NCERT textbooks, not only in history but in all subjects; therefore, the NCERT considered it prudent to use the existing textbooks until the new NCF provides with a detailed plan and advice for a comprehensive revision of the books and the syllabus of our school education.

In any event, rationalisation, filling up gaps, moving `away from Delhi-centrism and updating textbook content is a continuous process; there have been several changes in history textbooks since the first edition of these books was published in 1966.

Is it fair to say that only one group of people has the right to rewrite textbooks? Textbooks written by an earlier group of historians underwent many changes and, were replaced in 2006, by books written by a new set of authors. One does not recall any controversy over these changes. Furthermore, if rewriting textbooks was such an undesirable activity, we would still be teaching books written by colonial historians in our schools.

Institutions such as the NCERT should be concerned about reducing syllabus stress on students in our schools. As Ram Manohar Lohia said, India's history is more than 10,000 years old; therefore, the writers would naturally agonise over what topics to choose for a textbook. Thus, much care is required to keep two things in mind: What is relevant for a 16-year-old and how many facts she can absorb from her textbooks in one year, and how evenly and rationally the facts of our history are presented to her.

The NCERT has clarified that the section removed from the Class XII history textbook on the Mughals was unnecessary, as these details are available in the textbooks of previous classes; additionally, these sections contained the political history of the Mughals, which may not be required for school students. This logic is reasonable because certain aspects of history or political science can be deeply investigated at the university level.

If the writers of the current history textbook felt the necessity of teaching schoolchildren about the generosity and tolerance of the Mughals, then it would be equally appropriate to expect stories of their religious fundamentalism. Facts are sacred, though interpretations may vary. This criticism of the changes is like claiming what was said in 2006 is the final word, and no changes can be made. This is an exclusivist argument for a civilisation that celebrates diversity and assimilation.

The present NCERT social sciences textbooks must update their content, improve the language to make it lucid for students to understand and enjoy, and reflect a meaningful pedagogy. What is not required is a sermon from those who may think they know it all. Instead, facts must be presented lucidly so that students can glean the knowledge they wish to acquire. Most importantly, academics and politicians must keep away from politicising school textbooks. The textbooks should tell students the stories of our past but not weave in half-truths and gaps by erasing vast chunks of history.

The Cholas, Cheras, Pandyas, Pallavas, the dynasties that ruled the Vijayanagara kingdom, the Ahoms and the mighty Marathas, their bravery and contributions, are marginalised or absent from our school textbooks.

History cannot be written on shaky and fabricated foundations. What has been constructed was a mythical and artificial unity based on a falsified history. The NCF is attempting—I endorse its efforts—to bring a plurality of voices and an independent scheme of more inclusive representations of the versions of marginalised and previously excluded histories.

We need to be more honest about our past and the facts. History represents the memory of civilisations, the acts of people, and the past; historians must present this memory carefully and faithfully for future generations. Textbooks must change as the curriculum needs to be continuously revised to address gaps and make them more relevant and inclusive for changing times, and this is what the NCF is doing.

This is in keeping with our civilisation's ethos, in the words of Thiruvalluvar, who held that adherence to truth is an essential quality in writing any text.

21

Tech-Driven Education in India: Bridging the Gap

India's growth story in recent years can best be visualised as a tale of 'two cities' told through the discourses of gaps, divides and disparities. The Covid crisis made these fault lines more visible and uglier. Much of the technological transformation underway in urban and metropolitan parts was spearheaded to create deliverables for the less fortunate counterparts in rural India. One major endeavour has been in the field of education. The paradigm shift began in 2014, where a courageous rediscovery of civilisational values of balance between tradition and modernity, realm and region, continuity with change, excellence with equity, and innovation with inclusion.

When personal contact and mobility became difficult, India took a giant leap towards creating a digitally empowered and inclusive society. The challenges were immense, and access to the Internet was low, especially in rural India. However, with 560 million internet subscriptions in 2018, up from 238.71 million in 2013, India is the second-largest internet subscription market in the world and could provide a conducive ecosystem for the technological market companies to innovate in the field of education.

Urban India benefited immensely from the mushrooming of edutech companies offering a wide spectrum of online educational services. The edutech market in India was about US$ 2.5 billion in 2020 and is estimated to increase fourfold in the next five years to reach about US$ 10.0 bn. During the Covid crisis, it was realised that schools must undergo digital transformation. Therefore, all efforts were made to make learning more inclusive and intuitive.

India has about 312,000 common service centres nationwide, providing 350 Internet-enabled services, including education. In 2020, during the Covid crisis, the *Diksha*—nation-one-digital-platform—was launched to hoist a large number of educational content published by NCERT, CBSE and others to give universal and uniform access to students across all states and union territories to quality knowledge. The portal has embedded technology for students with visual and hearing impairments. Video recordings of over 2,000 textbooks have been uploaded on the portal and can be accessed in 31 Indian languages.

India's tech-driven education has ensured digital access and inclusion for children and students in the remotest parts of the country. Edutech platform 'first-in-class' flags its social values and has signed an MoU with Rotary India Literacy Mission to create the largest free edutech initiative in India and worldwide. The initiative was taken to mark India's 75th Year of Independence-*Azadi ka Amrit Mahotsav*; nothing could be more significant than dispelling the darkness of ignorance.

Many non-profit organisations have taken the initiative to bridge the digital divide by empowering teachers with technology such as AI-enabled WhatsApp Chatbot. The interactive chatbots helped teachers adopt and learn digital skills for teaching and learning purposes.

Many Indians can read and write in only one of India's more than 30 official languages. They cannot access the information on personal computers and laptops with English keyboards. Several Indian software developers have extended the reach of information and education to the Indian masses in local languages.

In 2020, India had one of the highest gender gaps in technology access. In 2015, only 10 per cent of internet users in India's rural areas were women. They suffered from information poverty due to the digital divide. However, smartphone usage among Indian women has increased phenomenally. India has a little more than 300 million households; smartphone usage is in about 200 million households, and at least one or more women users in each household.

Internet became handheld through the use of smartphones, trickling down to villages. Digital technology facilitated formal education and contributed immensely to skill-building in the informal sector. People learned new skills from Internet-enabled devices, became self-employed, and ran small businesses, which proved to be a lifesaving opportunity during COVID-19. India's contribution to ensuring inclusiveness is illustrated by the falling costs of data. India is the second largest smartphone user in the world, and the cost of data is among the lowest and has come down to INR 0.10 per GB.

One major concern in India's education sector has been the rising cost, and several Indian students opt for studying in countries like Ukraine and others to get professional education at affordable cost. Edutech companies provide digital access to quality education and smart governance options, reducing the institutions' overhead costs. Open Learning is a successful example of offering affordable education and has broken the boundaries to deliver education to the learners' doorstep. It offers a flexible learning model blended with online education and social tools like Moodle, WhatsApp and others. Moreover, it strives to embed audio and video-recorded lectures in online applications, facilitating the teaching and learning process for educators and learners.

India aims to become a major education hub with tech-driven content creation and dissemination within an inclusive, multidisciplinary framework. In 2021, India broke the Chinese record of having the largest number of unicorn start-ups in one year; edutech start-ups have a sizeable presence. Moreover, with new technologies like AI and blockchain, learning is accelerated, and careers are transformed.

After the COIVID-19 experience, the new normal is beset with greater comfort and confidence in online educational platforms. The students favourably weigh the cost-benefit analysis and flexibility of online courses vis-à-vis traditional campus learning. Online learning platform Coursera reported 49 per cent growth from students in India over the past 12 months, illustrative of the country's booming demand for online higher education. By June 2022, India had become the second largest market after the US, with over 24.6 million course enrolments. Coursera also cooperates with 1,100 campuses across India, co-creating courses for its students. They have report accessing more than 1.5 million learners and 14.1 million course enrolments since January 2020. According to the Bengaluru-based market research firm RedSeer, the online higher education market is estimated to grow from 90 million individuals in 2020 to 133 million individuals by 2025.

India is in a take-off phase of digital adoption, being the second fastest digitising country among the emerging and mature digital economies. It is set to become a global digital leader. A range of e-learning apps has increased and captured significant market share. There are innovative experiments in interactive learning through problem-solving assignments and elaborate discussions and feedback during online classes.

Among the existing challenges are connectivity and limited bandwidth. Internet penetration is usually associated with greater social progress in a nation. In this context, despite the existing challenges of not having uniform or universal access to the Internet, the sheer growth of Internet usage and enabled devices speaks volumes about the strides India has made in the last few years in bridging the gaps.

Education would be a major collaborative multilateral vertical in India's Presidency of G20 because it touches people's lives directly and thus has the potential to build stronger cooperation between the G20 member-states. India can help G20 member-states and other low and middle-income countries reimagine and reinvent their educational ecosystems, taking a leaf from its own National Education Policy 2020 and digital and technological transformations and in an Open Tech Model that promotes lifelong learning opportunities in a blended approach. India can showcase to the world its knowledge systems that promote sustainability and the ability to reinvent crises into learning opportunities. India's commitment to making G20 multilateral collaboration promote learning opportunities is illustrated by a special university connect event that virtually brought together students from 75 universities across the country on 1 December 2022, marking the first day of India's G-20 presidency. The *Amrit Kaal* is inclusive and innovative, leading both internally and internationally in the world that it sees as *Vasudhaiva Kutumbakam* (Thc world is onc family).

Nari Shakti
(Women)

22

Women Empowerment: Less Remembered Legacy of Dr Ambedkar

On April 14, we celebrate the 133rd birth anniversary of modern India's greatest statesman and social and economic reformer, Bharat Ratna Dr BR Ambedkar. His vision must be seriously studied as it addresses many issues still challenge an inclusive and equitable order. The vision of Nari Shakti and women-led development is central to the concept of *Amrit Kaal* and Viksit Bharat 2047. The Uniform Civil Code is also a tribute to this visionary leader of modern India—a common civil code was one of Babasaheb's dreams. Prime Minister Narendra Modi pays this tribute to the tallest leader and greatest icon, Dr BR Ambedkar. The recognition of women's autonomy and agency in certain matters contrasts with historical patriarchal norms of the past centuries that often have marginalised women's ownership and control over assets. Dr. BR Ambedkar, the father of the Constitution, a true social reformer, and a foremost feminist of independent India, was among the few luminaries of his time who passionately advocated for women's rights and empowerment.

"I measure the progress of a community by the degree of progress which women have achieved," noted Ambedkar. While his thoughts and actions on women's empowerment were numerous, this single line encapsulates how revered and fundamental he believed women to be in society and the nation. Despite historical accounts and subsequent analyses often limiting his efforts to uplift marginalised groups, including the Dalits, this perspective fails to do justice to Ambedkar's profound contribution to women's empowerment. Unlike some in the Left and ultra-liberal circles, who may view social justice as a political tool for gaining power and dividing society, for Ambedkar, social justice was a cardinal value for which he dedicated his lifetime, fighting for through his words and actions. His commitment to the progress and empowerment of women underscored the depth of his vision for a just and equitable society that extended beyond the boundaries of caste or class.

Among his many notable works, *Riddles of Hinduism* reflects Ambedkar's insightful meditations on women's rights, a topic often overlooked by many of his contemporaries and predecessors. While the fight against external adversaries, particularly British colonialism, was a prominent focus in India's freedom struggle, Ambedkar recognised another battle against domestic evils such as casteism and gender-based discrimination. In his writings, Ambedkar delved into the root causes of women's backwardness in Indian society during his time. He concluded that discrimination, coupled with societal ills like sati, child marriage, dowry, and restrictive marriage rites, hindered women from gaining education and led to their seclusion from the mainstream. Ambedkar's deep dive into ancient texts revealed that women's rights were not always curtailed; they were upheld graciously, except in certain texts, particularly the *Manusmriti* (laws of Manu). In one of his writings, Ambedkar emphasised, "Knowledge and learning are not for men alone...[but] essential for women too... [to bring change] educating girls is very important."

While pondering over such issues, the significance of education emerges as a pivotal force for societal advancement, with particular emphasis on providing equal educational opportunities for both males and females. The insights gleaned from the works of Dr BR Ambedkar underscore this, highlighting the transformative potential of education in addressing gender disparities and fostering inclusive development. Ambedkar's advocacy for women's education reflects his profound recognition of its role in dismantling entrenched inequalities. In his extensive writings, particularly in Volume Three of his collected works, Ambedkar offers incisive critiques of practices such as polygamy and concubinage, shedding light on the challenges faced by women within various cultural and religious contexts.

By comparing and contrasting these practices, Ambedkar not only condemns them but also illuminates how caste discrimination intersects with the treatment of women. This nuanced analysis underscores the multifaceted nature of gender inequality and the enduring struggle for women's rights in India. Ambedkar's insights serve as a poignant reminder of the complex interplay between social norms, cultural practices, and systemic discrimination, emphasising the need for comprehensive approaches to address gender disparities. By advocating for education and challenging regressive practices, Ambedkar contributed to the ongoing dialogue surrounding women's rights and social justice in India, leaving a lasting legacy that continues to inspire transformative change.

Undoubtedly, history illustrates that Ambedkar was a masterful intellectual and a man of action. Beyond his theoretical meditations, he made significant contributions to the upliftment of women. His contribution extends to the Mines Maternity Benefit Act, where he played a key role in drafting the legislation, ensuring equal pay and rights for coal mine workers. However, his most extraordinary contribution was his pivotal role in drafting the Hindu Marriage Bills, which later evolved into four Acts. These Acts should also be understood in the context of challenges independent India faced with integrating diverse Indian states into a unified nation, which meant the challenge of reconciling the varying legal codes, including those governing Hindu law. The four Acts granted women unprecedented agency in shaping their lives and achieving equal societal status. These legislative efforts granted women the right to inherit property, the ability to seek divorce (and maintenance), the legal authority to adopt a child, and the position of the natural guardian for their children. These fundamental measures laid the foundation for women's empowerment in independent India.

Thus, Ambedkar summed it up perfectly when he said that progression of a society should be gauged by the status of its women. Encouraging women to assert their equality within marital relationships and advocating for their education and empowerment are fundamental to societal advancement. This echoes the broader movement towards gender equality and women's empowerment that gained momentum in India with the likes of Ambedkar, who not only led by his words but also by his actions. Today, the efforts of the Modi government, encapsulated in the call for women-led development, stand on the foundations laid by Ambedkar and many others. *Nari Shakti* plays a crucial role in developing a progressive India. Although challenges remain, the last decade was genuinely transformational for women's status and ability to choose. Moving forward, as the journey towards a more equitable and just society continues, the contributions of Ambedkar, one of the foremost feminist statesmen of independent India, should be remembered and celebrated.

23

Draupadi: Feminist of Bharat

Is feminism merely a Western, left-wing and Woke concept of looking at gender in binaries? In the *Bharatiya* context, feminism is as old as our civilisation itself. That is 8,000 years, as carbon dating has proved, and the concept of the Mother Goddess is the idea of gender as balance and harmony in a nature-centric cosmos and not as a binary opposition to an anthropocentric world. These stories need to be retold, reimagined, and reconstructed. These stories, and particularly the female characters became the victims of patriarchy, reducing them to convenient embodiments of conventionality, rendering them mind-blowingly retrograde. Despite their powerful individual stories, the women characters from our mythology have been largely ignored. Sadly, it is this prejudiced interpretation of mythology that has, in many ways, shaped our concepts about the women of our society. But we can use these same stories to deconstruct these forgotten or distorted characters and employ them as a creative means to question and contest these stereotypes.

For decades, many Indians have dismissed our culture and history in pursuit of recognition from the West. This self-loathing dismissal of our history and culture has caused historical amnesia, and coupled with wilful ignorance, it has plagued India's understanding of its civilisational past. Some of this ignorance may be benign, but much of it is deliberate and malicious, leading to a negative view of our cultural heritage. The idea of the rule of the people or the concept of justice and gender equality is not exclusive to the West. It is even more erroneous to believe that the world was ignorant of such concepts until Western thinkers introduced them. India and many other civilisations have long grappled with these ideas and significantly contributed to their development.

Feminism in Ancient India

India has a rich tradition of *Nari Shakti* manifesting themselves through merit and courage, challenging the evils and injustices in the system. Draupadi (or Panchali) in the Mahabharata stands out as an original feminist figure in Indian history, known for her unyielding defiance. She emerges as a symbol of resilience amidst egregious indignity. Yet, she is not the sole exemplar of feminism within Indian culture. Sita, from the Ramayana, also embodies feminist ideals, albeit in a more nuanced manner. As one of the earliest examples of a single mother, Sita challenges traditional gender roles, although her character is often viewed through a more conformist lens.

As such, the notion of women breaking glass ceilings in ancient India was not an exception but the norm. Throughout history, women have excelled as mathematicians, philosophers, and scholars of Vedic literature, challenging the belief that feminism and gender equality are Western imports. It is both appalling and demeaning to suggest that India had to borrow these concepts from the West. Instead, India's rich cultural heritage boasts a long tradition of strong, empowered women who have contributed significantly to society, underscoring the fallacy of such assertions.

Draupadi, the Feminist

Draupadi, a figure entrenched within the rich tapestry of Indian history, society, and consciousness, embodies an intriguing complexity. She epitomises a duality symbolic of the human experience: at once womanly, compassionate, and generous, yet capable of standing up for herself against those who wrong her. The indignity inflicted upon Draupadi during the Mahabharata was a harrowing episode that reverberated throughout the Mahabharata and Indian society and history. Her defiance in the face of such adversity offers several consequential takeaways.

Firstly, her vocal condemnation of the injustice she endured was unprecedented. In the royal court, where she was wronged, Draupadi fearlessly confronted the elders and noblemen, piercing through their silence with a resounding call for accountability. Remarkably, she did so not with vitriol or obscenity but with masterful articulation steeped in sarcasm and irony. Through her words, she skilfully underscored the hypocrisy of their allegiance to King Dhritarashtra and Prince Duryodhana, juxtaposed against their moral and ethical duties. Draupadi's courageous interrogation of their misplaced loyalties resonates as a timeless reminder of the importance of moral integrity over blind obedience.

Secondly, Draupadi's words and actions are a poignant reflection of Indian culture and society, especially when it veers onto a misguided path of unjust behaviour. Amid societal turmoil, she emerges as a beacon of rectification, boldly confronting wrongdoing and advocating for justice. Thus, it was not just male figures who sought to bring about change in society in a positive manner; women also made invaluable contributions. Draupadi's refusal to remain silent in the face of such transgressions underscores her role as a societal redeemer, committed to steering her community towards the path of righteousness.

Thirdly, Draupadi's defiance extends beyond the personal realm to challenge broader gender hierarchies. Her anger, courage, and unwavering determination serve as a powerful resistance against the objectification of women. She transformed her traumatic episode into the manifestation of Nari Shakti, showcasing her indomitable spirit and resilience in the face of adversity.

Finally, Draupadi's story exemplifies the active role of women in shaping history and society. Her ordeal is pivotal, shedding light on the broader injustices women face and delineating the line between good and evil. Her steadfast refusal to accept her fate becomes a rallying cry for gender equality, inspiring others to assert their rights and demand justice. As Lord Krishna also elucidates, Draupadi's episode transcends the individual concerns of the Pandavas; it addresses the broader concerns of women and upholding Dharma in society. Draupadi's narrative thus offers a tale of personal triumph and a compelling catalyst for societal transformation.

Still Relevant

In contemporary society, echoes of Draupadi's struggle persist. The pervasive fear of women who assert their rights continues to permeate sections of society. Draupadi is often reduced to simplistic associations with polyandry or public humiliation, obscuring the profound significance of her narrative. This reluctance to confront Draupadi's true legacy mirrors a broader societal hesitance to address entrenched issues of domestic violence, abuse, and gender inequality. Despite notable strides made by some women across various domains, the persistent prevalence of these issues underscores the urgent need for societal introspection and reform.

It is a feminist civilisation where the triumph of the feminine is celebrated during Dussehra, and the most powerful portfolios are with female deities in Indra's cabinet, and to top it all, male Gods are named after their spouses—*Sitapati, Umapati, and Lakshmipati.* In celebrating *Draupadi*'s courage and resilience, we acknowledge her as a quintessential symbol of women's strength and a potent catalyst for societal transformation. By doing so, we honour *Draupadi*'s legacy and pave the way for a more inclusive and equitable society.

24

Women's Issues are not a Matter of Politics

Women's issues and feminism are universal, but does one hegemonic narrative of the Left and Liberal Westerners define all? There needs to be a celebration of diversity and multiple narratives. Bharat is a civilisational state long before most—a continuity of 8,000 years that has several perspectives that have been marginalised even in India. Is it ignorance or agenda-setting by Western-educated elites after Independence? Whatever the reason, this is a huge marginalisation of a feminist civilisational state, where the Pancha Pativratas are celebrated for breaking the rules, and the male Gods are known by their spouses, *Umapati* (Lord Shiva), *Lakshmipati* (lord Vishnu), and *Sitapati* (Lord Rama).

Draupadi (The wife of the Pandavas), the first feminist; *Sita* (The wife of Lord Rama), the first single mother; *Savitri* (Known for her devotion and determination), who defeated the Lord of Death by her logic and argument; *Saraswati* (The goddess of knowledge), who redefined marriage and childbearing; and several more. All this has been ignored, demeaned, or cancelled. Western narratives on women are seen in binaries and opposition.

Bharatiya narratives are not binaries but concentric circles of balance and harmony with the larger nature and cosmos. Hence, the Western binary lens distorts realities in Indian society. Several sociologists believe that the advent of organised religions of uniformity led to the rise of patriarchy.

How then can then the same binary lens be used for Bharat? Archaeology and carbon dating have proven that our civilisation was older and more advanced when the West was still picking stones. In fact, we were outward looking, which demolishes the myth of the Aryan invasion theory, constructed on interpretations and conjectures rather than facts. The issue of women's rights has been a prominent and enduring aspect of political discourse in the Western world over the past century.

As such, duly informed profoundly by our history, where we stand today regarding women's rights raises critical considerations about progress or regression and the lessons learned. Assessing the contemporary situation necessitates an honest reflection on whether the appropriate lessons from history have been absorbed or if there has been a divergence in the wrong direction. These questions should be central to the discourse among intellectuals, historians, and contemporary authors grappling with women's rights issues. Unfortunately, such clarity and honesty are seldom found, especially within today's political discourse.

Since Independence, women in India have faced numerous challenges, although positive developments have also occurred. Sadly, such instances of the advancement of women's rights in the last seven decades have been limited. Contrasting this with the last decade of the Indian Republic reveals a remarkable difference.

The period has seen an array of policies and initiatives that empower and educate women, fostering a path towards self-sufficient womanhood. The transformative initiatives of the past decade reflect a positive trajectory, indicating that substantial strides have been made towards addressing and enhancing women's rights in contemporary India.

Assessing the situation of women in India today involves considering multiple metrics, and one crucial aspect is their ability to choose and pursue diverse fields. Women's participation in science, technology, the military, business, trade, artistic endeavours, and other domains illustrates the expanding ability of women to choose and excel in various professional spheres. We see several 'first female' landmarks in different organisations, ranging from Jawaharlal Nehru University getting the first female VC to India getting the first female Defence, Finance and Foreign Ministers.

These are no ordinary examples but are representative of women's increased participation in the workplace. For the first time, women are increasingly participating as managers and leaders. It's also essential to recognise that the trajectory of women's rights today, encapsulated under Prime Minister Narendra Modi's clarion call of 'women-led development', is distinct from the radical feminist movements in the West.

Unlike approaches in postcolonial societies that insist on dividing genders, today's empowerment philosophy in India focuses on embracing and fostering inclusivity and acceptance. The emphasis is not on empowering and supporting one gender at the expense of another but on creating an ecosystem where all can coexist and function harmoniously. The government explicitly acknowledges and draws attention to India's civilisational heritage, rooted in thousands of years of learning, which views women as *janinis* (creators).

Yet, what remains concerning is that despite efforts to create an inclusive ecosystem for women's empowerment, there are still instances where a regressive mentality seeks to suppress women and promote divisive identity politics. Interestingly, support for such anti-women agendas often masquerades as 'Liberal Woke' ideas. Internationally, there are instances like the support within the Western universities for Hamas and its atrocities.

The October 7 attacks, regardless of the complex Israel-Palestine conflict, should have prompted unanimous condemnation for the blatant disregard and violation of women's rights and honour. But strangely enough, all those who portray themselves as a beacon of truth and social justice warriors are nowhere to be found. Instead, they stand on the side of Hamas. Back home, the recent situation in *Sandeshkhali* (West Bengal), where allegations of sexual atrocities against women and land grabbing by local Trinamool Congress leaders have emerged, is deeply concerning.

The ongoing violence and lack of remedial measures go beyond issues of law and order; they speak to the erosion of the social contract between the state government and the public. The state government, entrusted with ensuring safety and prosperity, appears to have become an exploiter. Despite revelations, primarily led by brave women protesters risking their lives, there has been a notable lack of action. The police, instead of apprehending the perpetrators, are obstructing independent fact-finding missions from entering the area.

The silence of the Woke adds to the politicisation of identities like caste, gender, and faith. This weakens the cause and its solutions for social and political justice. It raises questions about how a party led by a woman could be so insensitive to sexual exploitation and go to great lengths to cover up these atrocities. Such actions are neither indicative of good leadership nor good politics. While political debates and discourses are inherent in democracy, the moral compass should never be allowed to go astray.

Issues related to women cannot be misused for political gains. Women, as the sacred thread of origin, deserve honourable existence, and playing politics with their honour and lives in the balance is morally reprehensible. As a society, we have witnessed the dark ages of foreign Muslim invaders, and it seems we are not learning the proper lessons from history. Sacrificing respect and societal values that historically placed women at the centre of political ploys and cheap tricks to secure votes is a disheartening trend.

The respect for women, their bodies, and their choices should not be subjects for debate or political manoeuvring; instead, they are fundamental cornerstones of a vibrant and prosperous society and nation. As we commemorate International Women's Day this year, we should reflect on our civilisation and the many brave women it has produced. By prioritising the dignity of women, we must actively work towards creating an ecosystem where women are leading the way towards progress and prosperity to *Viksit Bharat* in 2047, with *Nari Shakti.*

25

Celebrating the Bharatiya Narrative on Feminism

All of us celebrate January 12 as the birth anniversary of Swami Vivekananda, while very few of us know it is also the birth anniversary of Jijabai, the mother of Chhatrapati Shivaji Maharaj and the architect of the Maratha empire alongside her son. There has been enormous negativity in our history textbooks about Chhatrapati Shivaji Maharaj.

The textbooks misrepresented Shivaji as an upstart robber, a marauder, and even a treacherous murderer while conveniently skipping or whitewashing the crimes of the invaders, such as rape, plunder and genocide, leading to a normalisation of such violent and cruel acts. It is time to reverse this type of narrative, call out biases and underline these gaps that require correction in both at the school and university level textbooks.

Feminism in the *Bharatiya* narrative is not in opposition to, or the either/or proposition, but one of harmony and balance. The concept of *Ardhanarishwar* (the Lord Who Is Half Woman), the balance and harmony between the masculine and the feminine, has been documented since the pre-Vedic times. The *Bharatiya* civilisation celebrates the Feminine, which is clear even with the portfolios in Indra's cabinet and the Feminine Trinity; the Five *Pativratas* (women who are devoted to their husbands) are those who broke the rules and male Gods known by the names of their spouses, like *Sitapati, Lakshmipati, Umapati,* and many more.

Across the villages in Karnataka, Kerala, and Tamil Nadu, chief Gramdevatas are goddesses. This is so different from the binary frameworks used by the West. Jijabai is one such figure who needs to be highlighted. Since childhood, Jijabai had seen the sufferings of her family and the public at large at the hands of Islamic invaders. Even though she was in severe suffering, Jijabai recognised that for the welfare of the common people, it was pertinent to raise Shivaji based on the Hindu ideas of *swaraj* (self-rule), *swabhimaan* (self-respect), and *swadesh* (native land).

Shivaji was just 14 years old when Shahjiraje handed him the jagir of Pune. Jijabai helped Shivaji redevelop Pune, which suffered massively at the behest of the exploitative policies of the Islamic rulers in the past. A mother trained in the art of warfare, especially in sword fighting and horse riding, moulded her son into a skilled warrior and instilled in him values such as modesty, truthfulness, oratory, vigilance, courage and fearlessness. She inspired in him the will to win and the dream of Swaraj.

As a single mother, Jijabai greatly influenced a young Shivaji. She encouraged him to read stories from Hindu scriptures to develop a strong moral compass in her son. She was also a skilled warrior and a horse rider. She was a brilliant administrator and guided her son, who built the Maratha empire that challenged the Mughals and even ruled Delhi for three decades. No story of Chhatrapati Shivaji Maharaj is complete without the story of his mother, Jijabai or Jijau, as she is fondly known in Maharashtra and was the embodiment of feminine power. Jijau's contribution to the making of Shivaji was second to none.

Shivaji, though the son of a nobleman, grew up among common people. Many of his childhood friends became his most trusted warriors, who later helped him achieve his dream of Hindavi Swaraj. Jijabai watched her son like a hawk, keeping him focused and away from distractions and vices. Her influence made him dream big, not just to be content with being a *jagirdar*. Having seen the plight of Hindu women under Islamic rule, Jijabai encouraged Shivaji to think about establishing an independent Hindu kingdom where the rights of Hindus would be respected.

She also taught him to be always protective of women and treat them with honour, a lesson Shivaji never forgot. When he established his kingdom, he harshly punished anyone who dared to dishonour or disrespect a woman, even a woman from the enemy camp.

Such was Jijau's bond with her son that she refrained from committing sati after her husband's death, even though it was the custom of the time. Her life's mission was fulfilled when she witnessed the grand coronation ceremony of Shivaji Maharaj, officially making him the first sovereign Hindu king of India since the fall of the Vijayanagara Empire. Barely twelve days after the coronation ceremony, Jijabai passed away at the age of 76 as a contented woman who had turned a dream of an independent Hindu kingdom into reality. Jijabai was known for her virtue, valour, and values, which she passed down to her illustrious son.

She championed the cause of *Swarajya* and helped inspire Shivaji Maharaj to unite the feuding Maratha factions to establish the "*Hindavi Swarajya* (Self-rule of Hindus)" which lasted until the 19th Century. Jijabai's stellar qualities—like her fiercely independent nature, her exemplary leadership skills, her commitment to Dharma, her intolerance of injustice, and her single-minded clarity—made Shivaji Maharaj into what he was, a visionary leader who continues to inspire generations of Indians.

This sacrifice, and contribution are seldom acknowledged. The sad part is that Nehruvian and the Left narratives of Independent India refused to acknowledge any dynasty other than the Delhi-centric ones and even whitewash the heinous crimes of Aurangzeb against the Marathas. A young monk, Swami Vivekananda, gave a comprehensive yet forceful narration of the life of Chhatrapati Shivaji. The important point to note here is how Shivaji Maharaj became a phenomenon in the national consciousness of India.

In 1645, in a letter written to Dadaji Naras Prabhu, Shivaji Maharaj first used the words *Hindavi Swarajya*. In a detailed essay on the concept, Bipin Chandra Pal (1858-1932) elaborated on its ancient origin and its modern relevance and, importantly, how the modern Indian polity inherited the term from the *Hindu Pad Padshahi* (Hindu Empire) established by Chhatrapati Shivaji: Shivaji sought the inclusion of the communities, that were in the periphery of the sociopolitical arena then, into the centre of *Swarajya*.

From the Hindu point of view, *Hindavi Swarajya* is a uniquely Hindu nation-building phenomenon. It did not start with Shivaji. It began long ago—right from the Vedic times—by emphasising human emancipation and realising the unity permeating all. This *Bharatiya* vision expressed itself through spiritualism ushering in organic social changes. Political forces anchored in Indian soil have always been tools for realising this fundamental vision of diversity in unity.

In modern times, this culminated in Shivaji Maharaj, giving him the mantric words *Hindavi Swarajya.* Social upliftment, military consolidation, spiritual diversity, and democracy stem from this seed-vision of Shivaji under the guidance of Jijabai and her indomitable *Sanskar* (values).

26

HT G20 Agenda: Nari Shakti to be a Driver of Change in India

India has made significant efforts to empower women and foster their participation in all aspects of society. Various policies and initiatives have been implemented to remove barriers and enable women to lead and contribute to the nation's development. The government's approach, focuses on egalitarianism, equity, and empathy, and has resulted in increased female literacy rates, financial independence, and improved health and well-being for women. India's commitment to women's empowerment is not only crucial for social justice but also reflects its role as a global leader.

If the considerable efforts of our *Nari Shakti* are combined to the hard work required to fulfil the dreams in this *Amrit Kaal*, it will reduce the effort needed and our deadlines will also be met. Our dreams will be more vivid, vivacious and resplendent, Prime Minister Narendra Modi noted in his 76th Independence Day speech. This statement captures the government's stance on women empowerment, while indicating foresight about the pivotal role that the government envisions for women.

Over the last decade, India has witnessed a remarkable shift towards empowering women and fostering their participation in the economy, society, and politics. Significant efforts have been made to create an environment where women could lead and spearhead the nation's development. While women's empowerment schemes were implemented by successive governments since the 1990s, the current approach is different as it seeks to remove various barriers—including mental, psychological, physical, economic, social, and political obstacles—by constructing narratives that foster an ecosystem characterised by egalitarianism, equity, and empathy.

To this end, several policies and initiatives have been introduced and adapted over time to address the evolving needs of women. Around a dozen major policies currently aim to empower women in education, entrepreneurship, skill development, health, well-being, and political representation. Through targeted interventions and awareness-raising efforts, the *Beti Bachao, Beti Padhao* scheme increased female literacy rates and reduced gender imbalances. Pursuing higher education and establishing businesses have become possible and accessible like never before. Schemes such as the Sukanya Samridhi Yojana (2015), Pradhan Mantri Mudra Yojana (2015), and Stand-Up India Scheme (2016) allowed women to gain financial independence while also becoming a contributor to India's economic development. The data on the growth of women-led enterprises, the narrowing gender gap, and increased credit to women entrepreneurs are a testament to changing realities.

The Pradhan Mantri Ujjwala Yojana was introduced to improve women's health, safety, and overall well-being in economically weaker households. By providing free LPG connections, the scheme effectively eliminates health hazards associated with traditional cooking methods, enabling women to pursue education, employment, and other opportunities. Meanwhile, the Pradhan Mantri Matru Vandana Yojana provides working women—who leave their jobs due to pregnancy–compensation for their wage loss.

Besides policy measures that impacted the lives of millions of women, the most significant change India witnessed was a societal renaissance that removed hidden barriers. The active government efforts, aided by rising consciousness among the Indian populace resonate with the renewed push for articulating and propagating *Bharatiya* (Indian) narratives. About women empowerment, there has been a reach into the hinterlands and remote tribal communities, manifested in the Prime Minister's regular recounting stories of women in his *Mann ki Baat* (Talk from the Heart) addresses. Moreover, there is a reinvigorated focus on broadening the knowledge base in Indian knowledge systems by incorporating diverse viewpoints and recognising the historical contribution of women from different regions of India. Finally, the Indic narratives that resonate with the themes of womanhood and core feminist values have enabled the connection of tradition with modernity, continuity with change, realm with region, and a theory with practice.

The Indic narratives that empower the feminine are highly relevant for Global South Alternatives. These narratives can be used as our civilisation values such as Draupadi as the first feminist, Sita as the first single mother, Kannagi as the first citizen activist, and Madhavi as the first poet. These narratives must be articulated extensively and researched. For these articulations, the use of science and technology are merely instruments, which are ineffective without developing an ecosystem that builds an egalitarian, equitable, and a non-discriminatory order, that will not have a lifelong and long-term impact.

India has recognised the universal significance of women's empowerment as a global issue, since it is evident that such concerns cannot be limited to national borders. As India gains increasing respect and recognition on the world stage, there is a need for the country to serve as a role model for others. Prime Minister Narendra Modi has demonstrated this awareness multiple times, most recently in his speech in Bali in November 2022, where he emphasised the indispensable role of women's participation in global development. He stressed prioritising women-led development in the G20 agenda, highlighting that global goals are attainable only with women's active involvement. This significant aspect has been prominently observed during India's chairmanship of the G20 this year. Recognising the importance of women empowerment internationally reflects India's commitment to driving a positive change both within its borders and globally.

In contrast to the Western approach of empowering women that remains limited to providing increased opportunities, the Indian approach of women-led development places women at the forefront of development, enabling them to take charge of their progress and play a leading role. India has come a long way in a short time, but the fact that there are still events where one sees the phrase 'first female' used should prompt better action and awareness. Women's empowerment is not just a matter of social justice; it is an inherent part of India's rich and vibrant civilisation. Although there is still progress to be made, the fact that India, as the world's oldest and largest democracy, is led by its first tribal woman as the head of State is a powerful testament to its commitment towards women-led development.

27

Mann ki Baat: A Bullhorn for Women's Empowerment

The use of a forgotten medium, the radio, revolutionised the popularity of *Akashvani* or All India Radio by a visionary Prime Minister in reaching the poorest of the poor in the far-flung remote areas. Prime Minister Narendra Modi hosted India's first 'visually enriched radio program', *Mann ki Baat*, on October 3 2014 to establish a 'dialogue with the citizens on issues of day-to-day governance'. Ever since, the radio program has discussed various issues that include, but were not limited to education, economy, foreign affairs, health, national security, politics, sanitation, start-ups, society and particularly, women. Over the last eight years, the government has vigorously campaigned for strengthening Nari Shakti across all segments of governance, including their participation in national defence. Whether congratulating women's success in sports or acknowledging their role in building an Ek Bharat, Shrestha Bharat, *Mann ki Baat* has been a critical platform for women's empowerment. But how exactly has *Mann ki Baat* engaged with women and related issues? Five major observations can be made in this regard.

Firstly, women have been a dominant focus in *Mann ki Baat*. Prime Minister Modi has spoken about the role of women in the context of history, politics, and their changing role in society. He has been a vocal advocate for revitalising the contributions of women in Indian history, particularly those from marginalised communities. A recurring theme in his talks is a high regard for women freedom fighters, educationalists, and social workers. For this reasons, Prime Minister has used the platform to draw attention to such notable yet overlooked figures of the past such as Savitribai Phule, whom he believes 'personifies the indomitable spirit of our *Nari Shakti*'.

Secondly, *Mann ki Baat* has addressed women both as a group and as individuals. As a group, Prime Minister Modi has discussed the macro directions in women's roles and their growing participation in the country's development. Here, the focus is mainly on collective concerns related to women, like entrepreneurship, health and nutrition, education, and leadership. A good example is an initiative in the Thanjavur district of Tamil Nadu known as *Tharagaigal Kaivinai Porutkal Virpanai Angadi* (Exhibition-cum-Sale of Handicrafts) which links 22 Self-Help Groups to sell several items like the Thanjavur doll, bronze lamps, bags, mats and toys. The initiative notably eliminates the middleman and helps women sell their products directly to clients. The Prime Minister hailed the group during the 89th edition of the show.

Meanwhile, the Prime Minister has addressed individual women from all parts of the country who have excelled in their fields and inspired others. This attention accorded to individual women is remarkable as it enables citizens (especially women) to reach out to the head of the government to share their stories and raise concerns. Prime Minister frequently mentions individual women by name to applaud them for initiatives that improved their lives and those of others around them. For instance, in the 98th edition of the show, he discussed an SHG run by Kamala Moharana of Kendrapada (Odisha), that makes sustainable baskets and mobile stands from milk pouches and plastics. Similarly, in the 21st episode, Prime Minister Modi praised Babita Rajput of Agrotha village (Madhya Pradesh), who mobilised other women in Agrotha to build a canal to bring water to a dried-up lake that threatened their survival.

Thirdly, *Mann ki Baat* helps to link women empowerment with the country's development. From the outset, the Modi administration has sought to change the scope and notion of empowering women by emphasising a shift from 'women empowerment' to 'women-led empowerment'. This shifted approach may appear inconsequential; however, it marks a fundamental change in how the government addresses women and women's issues. Instead of viewing women merely as beneficiaries of the development agenda, it has made women a 'critical prerequisite' for development. Mann ki Baat is a critical component in delivering this message.

Fourthly, through *Mann ki Baat*, Prime Minister Modi has sought to reach out to the country's non-women populace to remodel women's roles in Indian society. In a recent episode, Prime Minister Modi exclaimed that the 'daughters of the country are raising the flag of their bravery'. He referred to this in the context of Group Captain Shalija Dhami (the first woman Air Force officer to receive a Command Appointment in a Combat Unit), Captain Shiva Chauhan (the first woman officer to be posted to Siachen), and the women-only platoon of peacekeepers at the UN Mission in Sudan and South Sudan. Similarly, he also commended the women who went to earthquake-struck Turkey as part of the National Disaster Response Force units. Such decisions underscore the government's intent of creating a separate space for women's societal role beyond that of homemakers.

Fifthly, through its numerous examples of women succeeding and bringing about change, *Mann ki Baat* has served as a publicising platform for the government's initiatives. The government has launched over a dozen women-specific policies over the last eight years, including *Sukanya Samriddhi* (Girl prosperity), *Beti Bachao Beti Padaho* (Save the Girl Child, Educate the Girl Child), Stand-Up India, Prime Minister *Jan Dhan Yojana* (People's Wealth Scheme), Prime Minister *Mudra Yojana* (Micro Units Development and Refinance Agency), Prime Minister *Matru Vandana Yojana* (Maternal Gratitude Scheme), *Sarvada Shaktishaali* (Always Empowered) Scheme. However, the government faces a significant challenge in making the public aware of such policies. Here, Prime Minister has used *Mann ki Baat* as an affordable and easily accessible instrument to reach the widest possible audience and inform them of government initiatives. Whether allowing girls in Sainik Schools or helping women start businesses, Prime Minister Modi has dedicated considerable time to publicising government policies and raising awareness.

In a nutshell, the Prime Minister's return to radio to reach out to people showcases that the government's focus is less on the projection of empowerment and more on delivery, wherein *Mann ki Baat* has been a bullhorn for women's empowerment. An issue to that international leaders lament is that achieving gender equality will take a long time, as many as 200 years, but in India, the Prime Minister has given a clarion call for *Nari Shakti* in the making of *Amrit Kaal*, India 100 at 2047. It is a major challenge and an opportunity to achieve together an Indic Civilisation that conceived gender not in binaries but as two parts of a whole, the concept of *Ardhanareshwar* (The Lord Who is Half Woman), a balance of male and female energies.

28

Towards an India Where Women Lead

The journey from India at 75 to India at 100 makes me think of many things. However, two things in particular captured my imagination: making higher education more Indo-centric and reducing the gender gap at the top. Even after 75 years of independence, women have a long way to go. The journey towards equality and equity, with inclusion is still long and tedious and seems to be a pipe dream.

Women's leadership in higher education and education-related decision-making bodies at the government level is largely absent as these remain male dominated clubs. Only seven of India's 54 central universities have women vice-chancellors. This is despite girls outnumbering boys in higher education admissions and women constituting more than 50 percent of entry-level university teaching positions. The situation is even worse for those from the reserved categories.

There are several reasons for this: Women need to multitask; marriage and family are still considered women's responsibilities; despite being qualified, women continue to be hobbled by the ruthless, identity-based politics that plague our higher education institutions. In addition, women must fight entrenched patriarchy and male hegemony. It takes a lot of courage, time, and energy to combat these social ills, and many women do not want to, as the fight can become dirty and time-consuming. The few who dare to fight are often maligned. A woman's assertiveness is seen as aggressiveness.

These inequalities are further confirmed by the 2022 World Economic Forum's Gender Gap Index. India's overall score has improved from 0.625 (in 2021) to 0.629, making its seventh-highest score in the last 16 years. It will take 132 years to reach gender parity, with the gap reducing only by four years since 2021. This is a dim prospect for a civilisational state that boasts of the elevation of the feminine.

We need to rediscover and reinvent our civilisational journey. The emancipation and empowerment of the Indian mind is the first step. We are disconnected and colonised in our thinking and scholarship. In the last 75 years, we have moved between self-hatred and self-loathing and imitating the West without understanding ourselves. It is time that we embark on this intellectual journey towards creating original knowledge that goes back to our roots. This journey is a must for every Indian who wants India to be a *Vishvaguru*. This is my vision for India at 100. Technology and other means are important, but they are just instruments and cannot replace the quality of the human mind.

Just consider the sad plight that we are in concerning the status of women, although the present government is doing its best to break various glass ceilings. For me, the glass ceiling needs to be broken is the intellectual slavery of the Indian mind, where all that is Western is good, and anything Indian is seen as being regressive and, therefore, bad. All events need to be secularised and the invaders need to be humanised.

In history, we often tend to celebrate of the valour of men who conquered cities through violence and forget the women's side of the story. Even though women generously populate our civilisational stories, there has hardly been any retelling of these stories from a feminine perspective until recently. We are a civilisation that has always elevated the feminine and celebrated the harmony of the masculine and the feminine in the image of *Ardhanarishwar*.

Goddesses represent the humanisation of various abstract values. In the concept of the *Tridevi*, *Parvati* represents power, *Lakshmi* represents fortune, and Saraswati represents knowledge. And unlike *Parvati*, who is the epitome of motherhood, Saraswati firmly asserts that she does not believe in marriage and love. She emphasises that it is more important to love yourself as an individual and love your work; unless you do that, you won't be a positive asset to society and the people around you.

Women characters are often misinterpreted. Take *Savitri*, who outwitted *Yama* (God of Death) with her determination and argument. Another politically strong person is *Tara*, (the wife of *Bali* and *Sugriva)*, who is the reason the *vanaras* (monkeys) become part of *Rama's* army. Looking at all these women, it is clear that they have been misinterpreted because of social pressure and ignorance. *Pativratas* are women who broke the rules. Which other tradition has this progressive, even revolutionary, narrative?

In one of the earliest recorded protests against a male-dominated world and society, *Draupadi*'s fight against injustice reflects one of the first acts of feminism—a fight for one's rights. In this case, avenging the wrongs inflicted on her was her right. She is exemplified as one of the earliest feminists, whether in terms of polyandry—regarded as a matter of censure by society, both then and now—or in terms of her thirst for revenge. Why can't Sita be seen as the first single mother?

Unless and until India becomes a norm-builder, we will go nowhere. We will imitate others while losing all our own. Higher education institutions must open themselves up to multiple Indic narratives because they represent the space where true liberation can begin in the mind. The emancipation and empowerment of women need to be fought for first at the level of ideas and narratives. The real battle for us lies at the level of the mind and intellect, from now until India in 2047.

India is a civilisational state that rests on the shoulders of women such as Sita, *Draupadi*, *Kannagi* and *Manimekalai*. They were unconventional, intelligent, strong-willed, and capable of making independent decisions and exercising autonomy. India at 100 will be where women will be able to reclaim and reconstruct such a strong civilisational heritage by leading the state from the front as leaders across all fields.

Social Issues

29

A New Dawn in the Northeast

The policy of divide and rule constructed by the post-colonial Nehruvian state used identity to create separate identities in the Northeast. This process was ahistorical, for as it overlooks the continuity of cultural influences of Vaishnavism and Shakti worship and practices. Tribal culture has continuities with *Bharatiya* culture rather than with those of the invaders. The colonial project was employed to construct a false consciousness; thus, it was easy to alienate and convert. Since 2014, a paradigm shift has taken place to unite the Northeast as an integral of the Indic civilisation state, where cultural diversity is celebrated as in all other regions and states.

The northeastern region of India is undergoing a landmark transformation. The government of Prime Minister Narendra Modi has sought the development of the eight states of the Northeast (referred to as *Ashtalakshmi* [Eight Laxmis]) through a 'whole-of-government approach' that is rooted in the dual objectives of establishing peace and stability while fostering the comprehensive development of the Northeast. The broader vision aims to transform the Northeast into a flourishing contributor to India's larger vision of *Viksit Bharat*.

Under the visionary framework termed '*Purvoday* (Eastern Dawn)', the government has formulated a strategy for the Northeast region anchored in three key principles: firstly, accelerating development for integration with the nation, highlighting the imperative of fast-tracking development initiatives to facilitate seamless integration of the Northeast with the broader national framework; secondly, dealing with conflicts to establish peace and stability, underscoring the importance of addressing and resolving conflicts as a fundamental prerequisite for sustained peace and stability; and thirdly, economic and cultural enrichment for development, emphasising the significance of cultural preservation and economic enhancement as integral to the overall development of the region. These principles collectively form the bedrock of a comprehensive approach to foster holistic growth and progress in the region. Measured against these normative standards, the raw facts about the region yield a decidedly positive and encouraging conclusion—there is a new dawn in the Northeast.

Peace with Security

Over the past decade, incidents of insurgency and casualties among civilians and security forces have reached the lowest levels. The improvements in the security situation from 2014 to 2023 are noteworthy, including a 73 per cent reduction in insurgency incidents, a 71 per cent reduction in security forces' casualties, an 86 per cent reduction in civilian deaths, and the surrender of over 8,900 extremists. The underlying approach is centred on building long-term peace to address persistent challenges. In 2023, agreements were signed with prominent groups such as the United Liberation Front of Assam (ULFA), the United National Liberation Front (UNLF), and the Dimasa Peace Accord. Earlier agreements, including the Tribal Peace Accord (Assam, 2022), Assam-Meghalaya Inter-State Boundary Agreement (2022), Assam-Arunachal Pradesh Inter-State Boundary Agreement (2022), Karbi Agreement (2021), Bru Agreement (2020), Bodo Accord (2020), and NLFT/SD Agreement (2019), have contributed to stabilising the region. Another significant milestone has been achieved in reducing unrest-prone areas in the Northeast governed by the Armed Forces (Special Powers) Act (AFSPA). It has been entirely removed in Tripura and Meghalaya. Currently, it operates in a limited capacity in Assam (four4 districts), Nagaland (four districts), Manipur (seven districts), and three districts in Arunachal Pradesh. These developments reflect a concerted effort to bring about lasting peace and stability in the region.

Economic Upturn

The past decade has witnessed remarkable growth in infrastructure development, improved connectivity, and increased per capita incomes across the region. Notably, there has been substantial growth in per capita income across various states. Manipur has witnessed a doubling of per capita income, while Mizoram stands out with a remarkable 3.2 times growth. Arunachal Pradesh and Tripura experienced an almost threefold (2.9 times) increase in their per capita Net State Domestic Product (NSDP) over the same period. Nagaland and Assam registered growth exceeding 2.5 times (see Figure). Although slightly more modest, Meghalaya still achieved an impressive 1.5 times growth in per capita income. These statistics underscore the positive economic trajectory in the region, with tangible improvements in the standard of living.

The Northeast region is experiencing increasing benefits from the Vibrant Village Program, with substantial budgetary allocations reflecting the government's commitment to development. The Ministry of Development of Northeastern Region (Ministry of Development of Northeastern Region) witnessed a significant budget increase, from INR 2,333 crore in 2014-15 to INR 5,892 crore in 2023-24, marking a remarkable 153 per cent growth. Infrastructure schemes have been instrumental, with the Prime Minister Development of Villages and Infrastructure in Northeastern Region Scheme allocating INR 1,500 crore. Several transformative projects are underway, including the National Ropeway Development Program—'*Parvatmala* (Mountain Garland)'—implemented in a Public-Private Partnership (PPP) mode for building eight ropeway projects spanning 60 km to boost connectivity in the Northeast and other hilly states. The *Bharatmala* (Bharat's Garland) Project, aiming to construct 5,196 km of roads, has completed 514 km. Sector-specific missions, such as the National Mission on Edible Oils—Oil Palm, the National Bamboo Mission, and the Majuli project, highlight the focused approach to diverse development needs.

Meanwhile, several capacity-building initiatives include two water supply projects totalling INR 118 crores. The Northeastern Development Finance Corporation Limited has substantially contributed by supporting 5,490 projects in microfinance, totalling INR 789 crores in sanctions and INR 622 crores in disbursements. The Sambhav Mission Mode Program, aimed at establishing 75 gram panchayats/village councils in 42 districts of 8 states in the Northeast, has enabled fundamental services to all citizens. Furthermore, in alignment with the climate agenda that the government is spearheading on the global stage, plans to revive 292 wetlands in the region have been formulated under the Northeastern Space Applications Centre. This multi-pronged approach reflects the government's commitment to holistic development, encompassing infrastructure, agriculture, and environmental sustainability in the Northeast.

A Real Change

Genuine challenges persist in the Northeast, a region that has been historically neglected and mismanaged since India's independence. Erroneous policies, which often sought division rather than unity, exacerbated the challenges of separatism through a lack of development and insufficient attention to regional issues, with petty politics further aggravated these challenges. However, the impact of the government's current strategy is becoming increasingly evident, marked by consistent peace and stability, reflected in declining insurgent activities, reduced inter-state border disputes, and substantial investments in development. The northeastern states are rapidly progressing towards realising the status of *Ashtalakshmi*, contributing significantly to the larger national narrative and emerging as an economic force. To put it differently, despite historical setbacks, the region is poised for positive transformation and increased integration into India's growth trajectory.

30

Transformed Kashmir is a Tribute to Dr SP Mukherjee

The Nehruvian state cancelled two great leaders, the founders of the *Bharatiya* Jan Sangh—Shyama Prasad Mukherjee (1901 to1953) and NC Chatterjee (1895 to1972). Does anyone in the post-independence generations know these leaders who were cancelled by the ecosystem of the Nehruvian state? SP Mukherjee, a brilliant speaker who challenged the Nehruvian state, was systematically marginalised, and the case of his death in custody in Jammu and Kashmir has raised several unanswered questions. The removal of Article 370 is a tribute to this great leader and martyr. He fought vehemently against the partition of Bengal, and if there is a state called West Bengal today, it is due to his courage to speak about the atrocities against Hindus.

In post-Independence India, Shyama Prasad Mukherjee, the founder of the Jan Sangh, emerged as a prominent and vocal critic of Article 370, advocating the end of the special status accorded to Jammu and Kashmir (J&K). His steadfast opposition was encapsulated in the famous line, "*Ek desh mein do Vidhan, do Pradhan aur do Nishan nahi* challenge (A country cannot have two constitutions, two prime ministers, and two emblems)." Removing the temporary Article is indeed a demonstration of courage of conviction of the present Government and a paradigm shift in finally uniting India.

Mukherjee, however, was not alone in recognising the potential dangers of a special status for J&K. BR Ambedkar, the visionary architect of India's Constitution, shared similar concerns. The initial draft he submitted had no provision for such special status. When Nehru's associate, N. Gopalaswami

Ayyangar, sought its inclusion, Ambedkar refused to attend the session, that passed the motion to include Article 370. Ambedkar strongly objected, "You want India to defend Kashmir, feed its people, give Kashmiris equal rights all over India. But you want to deny India and Indians all rights in Kashmir. I am the Law Minister of India, and I cannot be a party to such a betrayal of national interests."

Article 370 Abrogated

The watershed moment of abrogation of Article 370 and the reorganisation of J&K realised Mukherjee's vision and honoured the legacies of stalwarts like Ambedkar and Sardar Patel, who considered such exceptions detrimental to India's unity. Provisions meant as exceptions could not and should not become norms or tools for anti-democracy elements. Despite this, sceptics persist in scrutinising and questioning the legitimacy of the changes resulting from this decision. Four years after the pivotal move, both tangible and intangible transformations have occurred in J&K. Tangible changes include improvements in infrastructure, agriculture, industry, and various socio-economic indicators.

Furthermore, progress is evident in irrigation projects, road infrastructure, and across sectors such as healthcare, tourism, and education, which are experiencing developments that previously remained unavailable to the people of J&K. The more noticeable consequence of the abrogation is an intangible transformation in the mindset of J&K that has created an environment conducive to progress and inclusivity, thereby shifting the atmosphere from hostility to a welcoming, constructive, and empowering environment. Home Minister Amit Shah succinctly highlights the change, noting that the youth of J&K are now "taking computers in their hands instead of stones."

Economy and Infrastructure

J&K's economic landscape has undergone an unprecedented transformation, with the Gross State Domestic Product (GSDP) rising significantly from INR 1 lakh crore in Financial Year (FY) 2014-15 to INR 227,927 crore in FY 2022-23. Notably, investments surged from INR 297 crores in FY 2019-20 to INR 2,153 crore in FY2022-23, totalling INR 5,319 crore between 2019-20 and 2023-24. The highest investment occurred in FY 2022-23, showcasing not only the economic growth of J&K but also its potential as an economic powerhouse contributing to the Indian economy.

Amidst broader political shifts, J&K's education system is also gaining attention, moving beyond separatism. Government investment is evident in increased educational infrastructure, with functioning colleges rising from 94 to 117, a 33 per cent growth over four years. Notably, prestigious institutions like one IIM, one IIT, and two AIIMS have enhanced higher education. Medical colleges have nearly doubled from four to seven, and 15 new nursing colleges have been established.

Farewell to Terrorism

The government's unwavering zero-tolerance policy against terrorism has yielded encouraging results, successfully dismantling the terror ecosystem and ushering in a sustained period of peace and stability in J&K for the first time since the 1990s. These collective efforts are visibly reflected in a notable decline in terror incidents, contributing to a congenial atmosphere. From 2018 to November 2023, there has been a significant reduction in terrorist-initiated incidents by 81.14 per cent. Civilian casualties have decreased by 76.36 per cent, and the number of security personnel killed in action has seen a reduction of 72.53 per cent. Notably, encounters have decreased by 74.60 per cent, signalling a shift from a heavy-handed approach. One of the most significant achievements is nearly eradication of stone-pelting incidents, dropping to zero in 2023 from 1,767 incidents in 2018. This demonstrates the effectiveness of the government's approach in curbing not only major security threats but also addressing incidents that could potentially escalate tensions in the region. The overall statistics underscore the transformative change in the security landscape of J&K.

Inclusive Development

The recent passing of the Constitution (J&K) Scheduled Tribes Order (Amendment) Bill, 2024, in the Lok Sabha is a noteworthy development that bestows Scheduled Tribe status upon tribal communities like Pahari, Padari, Koli, and Gadda Brahmin. This legislative move underscores the government's commitment to acknowledging and uplifting marginalised communities in J&K. Post-abrogation, another fundamental change in J&K that revolves around women's improved status and opportunities. Earlier, women faced lamentable conditions due to inadequate laws and poor implementation, subjecting them to patriarchal constraints. Restrictions on life decisions, such as marrying outside Kashmir, deprived them of domicile privileges. The abrogation has empowered women to retain property even if they marry outside the state. By dismantling discriminatory practices, it has expanded their choices. Moreover, the emerging economic opportunities in J&K enable women to enter the workforce and contribute to Prime Minister Modi's clarion call for women-led development.

In essence, J&K has transformed from a liability to a value addition simply because the government unapologetically removed discriminatory provisions from the Constitution. This, in turn, defanged vested interests that hindered the people of J&K from fully integrating with the rest of India. Post-abrogation, the government's interventions, rooted in the spirit of 'Sabka Saath, Sabka Vishwas', have led to inclusive development and steered J&K towards a collective journey of progress and trust-building while fostering J&K's contribution to *Viksit Bharat*. Finally, it is a tribute by Prime Minister Modi, the tallest spokesperson of the story of democracy, to one of the cancelled makers of the Indian Constitution, Dr Shyama Prasad Mukherjee, by the Nehruvian state.

31

The Shadow of Violence: Confronting Issues in Manipur and Beyond

Violence has been erupting in different states, which seems to be pre planned and a method seems to exist in the madness. Manipur in May and June, Haryana now. Was Manipur preplanned as to prove that the false propaganda that India is unsafe for its minorities and women, exactly when Prime Minister Modi was visiting the US. Now every year this yatra takes place in Haryana why this year and now before the G20 summit in Delhi and to dent India's image of being a favoured as an investment destination. What surprises one is timing and the way ecosystem echoes it collectively. All this is with the fear of the 2024 Lok Sabha elections and its results. Rather such preplanned attacks will be detrimental to those who are echoing and supporting this violence.

The selective uproar against the rape of women is something that leads to politicization of a heinous crime. Rajasthan has the highest number of rape cases. So why is there no condemnation of the state by the ecosystem? Rape anywhere is to be condemned. Is there anything secular if it happens in Opposition ruled states? This has to change.

The continuing crisis in Manipur is a stark reminder of the numerous domestic and foreign challenges India grapples with in the Northeast. Since gaining independence, New Delhi has faced the formidable task of integrating the North Eastern states into the nation. Independent India has faced a host of complex issues: encompassing security concerns, developmental hurdles, narcotics trade, illegal activities, ethnic violence, unlawful immigration, cross-border terrorism, religious conversions, and tribal conflicts. Each of these challenges is profound in its own right, and successive governments in New Delhi have encountered the daunting combination of these issues across almost all states in the region.

Despite witnessing remarkable growth in infrastructure development, improved connectivity, and increased per capita incomes over the last decade, the shadow of these challenges looms large. Table 1 shows the commendable growth in per capita income across these states. For example, Manipur's per capita income doubled from INR 39,762 to INR 84,345. At the same time, Arunachal Pradesh and Tripura experienced a threefold increase in their per capita NSDP within the same period. Moreover, violence related incidents had significantly decreased, leading to the removal of vast areas from the purview of the Armed Forces (Special Powers) Act (AFSPA), leaving only a handful of districts still affected.

Yet, security issues remain potent disruptors and challenges to state authority. In addition, there is an increasing challenge coming from transnational crimes, particularly drug trade and smuggling. While these crimes may initially be viewed as petty, their ramifications are far-reaching, laying the groundwork for more severe dangers like terrorism, organized violence, and societal decay. The border villages and towns in the Seven Sister States bear the brunt of the insidious influence of the infamous Golden Triangle. Many studies have pointed out how Manipur and Mizoram, in particular, have become parts of the notorious Golden Triangle. This has resulted in the influx of large quantities of arms into these states, ostensibly to protect drug trafficking routes. However, these very weapons eventually end up being misused by the locals, settling personal rivalries with dire consequences for the communities. The situation exacerbates existing societal tensions, and the unholy nexus between drugs and arms gives rise to escalated violence. Minor conflicts are manipulated and given ethnic, racial, or tribal colour, deflecting attention from the core issue of drugs while allowing the illicit network to flourish. As a result, these states have witnessed an alarming per capita armament, further perpetuating the cycle of violence. Both sides are equally to blame and with external actors like China and the drug cartels involved.

Compounding the problem is the deeply polarized nature of politics in India, which hampers constructive policy debates and discussions in the region. Moreover, the involvement of the Church and evangelical groups that have transnational linkages has added fuel to the fire, disturbing social harmony. As a result, religious identities have become more pronounced over the years, with incidents of forced conversions rising. While some may interpret these conversions as religious freedom, it is evident that they often involve unscrupulous methods involving coercion and economic incentives.

In the face of such vexing problems that have plagued the region, the path to viable solutions remains fraught with difficulty and cannot be achieved overnight. The region's vulnerability lies in its porous borders, facilitating infiltration and smuggling. Remarkably, a mere five per cent of these borders are presently fenced, underscoring the pressing need for action. As such, one proposed solution is the implementation of advanced smart borders, which promises to effectively keep potential threats and ensure the security of its citizens. Illegal migration poses a formidable challenge for countries transitioning from developing to developed economies, enticed by the plethora of economic opportunities. From a broader perspective, the Citizenship Amendment Act (CAA) can be perceived as a generous measure driven by the aim to strike a delicate equilibrium between safeguarding the rights of Indian citizens and extending refuge to those seeking safe haven from their home countries. Critics, however, tend to criticize such decisions from a moral standpoint, often overlooking the complexities of public policy-making.

Nevertheless, installing robust borders is necessary to establish law and order and foster a secure environment for all citizens. Striking a balance between compassion and pragmatic policy-making is vital to finding lasting solutions that safeguard the well-being of the region and its people.

An additional measure of concern that demands immediate attention is the need to tackle half-truths and misinformation that pervade reporting on the region. Regrettably, economic success stories that genuinely impact the lives of the public often go underreported and fail to circulate widely. Conversely, negative incidents receive undue attention from foreign media, painting a skewed image of India and Indians. Manipur serves as a grim reminder of the challenges we face, transcending ideological boundaries. Condemnation of such events is imperative, as is their exposure, but exploiting them as political tools exhibit insensitivity and undermines the gravity of the situation. It is not just an internal security issue but also national security due to geopolitical reasons of the drug infested Golden Triangle and the role of China funding the extremist groups with light weapons and small arms.

Drawing inspiration from the words of former US President John F. Kennedy, who urged citizens to ask not what their country can do for them but what they can do for their country, we must collectively seek ways to rectify the issues in Manipur and the broader Northeast. There is a need for dialogue, empathy and education. More than ever, there is a need to listen to others and find solutions. The youth of the country need to be sensitized about issues, concerns, and challenges that India faces. The change we all seek would happen not by screaming and spitting angry jibes but by reaching out for solutions. By combating misinformation, one sided propaganda and demonising the other, holding the truth in high regard, and taking concrete actions, we can pave the way towards a brighter future for Manipur and the entire Northeast. It takes all sides to be committed to peaceful resolutions.

The recent violence and harrowing incidents in Manipur are an unpleasant wake-up call, underscoring the deep-seated divisions and fault lines that persist within our nation and society particularly at the critical crossroads of national and regional security. It is no secret that malicious actors will exploit these vulnerabilities to our detriment. One should remember a single moment of discord can shatter decades of hard-earned harmony. In these challenging circumstances, the responsibility falls upon us to rectify the situation and ensure that such tragedies never befall anyone again. Women, the creators of life, hold a special place in the Indic culture, a testament to our cherished diversity. It is imperative that we move beyond mere politics and empty virtue signalling, instead focusing on tangible actions that bring about positive change. Rather than playing the blame game, we must urgently address the root problems and take decisive measures to resolve them. By standing together and working collectively, we can ensure that the spectre of tragedy is banished and our nation moves forward in strength and solidarity.

32

Science and Spirituality in Indian Knowledge Systems: Learning from Swami Vivekananda and Ranganathananda

The *Bharatiya* narrative architecture perceives knowledge as holistic and not in binaries of the Cartesian Divide, where the pursuit of science and technology was closely intertwined with spirituality. There was no opposition between the Hindu way of life and the pursuit of knowledge. It was never in binary of science versus religion; it is science and religion together. Temples were built scientifically with amazing technological skills. One sees the engineering marvels and scientific facts in many temple architecture, which requires systematic research.

There is a connection of science of the individual, both from within and without, the environment and the cosmos. Since outlining the visionary agendas of *Amrit Kaal* and, more recently, *Viksit Bharat* 2047, Prime Minister Narendra Modi has been insistent on ideas and themes aimed at transforming India into a developed nation. The government has undertaken multiple policies and initiatives to pursue these objectives. For the realisation of the *Amrit Kaal* in *Viksit Bharat* 2047, the development of the *Bharatiya* narrative architecture through its Gyan Parampara or knowledge systems is imperative.

Understanding *Bharatiya Gyan Parampara*

In its primary sense, the Indian Knowledge Systems (IKS) or *Bharatiya* Gyan Parampara seeks to transmit ancient knowledge and traditions into modern contexts for appropriate integration into contemporary applications. This approach entails acknowledging the wisdom of the past, drawing inspiration and lessons from it while preserving India's rich heritage. Indeed, IKS encompasses a broad spectrum of works that can be viewed through the lens of both science and spirituality. However, what distinguishes IKS is its holistic perspective, where neat categorisations are often transcended.

India's contributions to various fields are immense and diverse, including architecture, astronomy, physics, engineering, fine arts, mathematics, metallurgy, medical science, surgery, navigation, and yoga. The philosophical contributions are equally substantial, extolling on the role of humans in society, the proper conduct of life, and their place in nature. Central to these philosophies is aligning oneself with the *Panchbhoots*, or the five elements of nature. This holistic approach underscores the interconnectedness of all aspects of existence and the importance of harmony with the natural world. For these reasons, IKS has become invaluable, and its dissemination to the public, particularly to the youth, has become essential.

The NEP 2020 recognises this and is working on its inclusion in the curriculum so that the youth can become aware of India's profound heritage of wisdom and knowledge practices. However, historians and intellectuals have fallen short in promoting the IKS, dispelling misconceptions about it, and giving due respect to the vast heritage neglected and sometimes denigrated due to a colonial mindset. In service of these efforts, let us examine Swami Vivekananda's and Swami Ranganathananda's contributions to understanding and appreciating the IKS.

Blending Science with Spirituality

The two doyens exemplify through their work how science and spirituality need not be antithetical but can be harmonious. They represent the essence of IKS by not accepting the knowledge of the past as given and unchangeable, which is a hallmark of the education system in Indian traditions. Everything, including religion, rituals, and practices must undergo rigorous examination through the traditions of *Tarka* (logic).

Vivekananda believed that science explored the external world, uncovering the laws of nature, while spirituality delved into the inner realms of consciousness, unveiling the mysteries of the self and the universe. He believed a holistic approach to knowledge was necessary, embracing empirical investigation and inner exploration. He encouraged scientists and spiritual seekers alike to broaden their perspectives and engage in a dialogue transcending disciplinary boundaries.

Likewise, Swami Ranganathananda fervently endeavoured to mend the apparent schism between science and spirituality, championing a harmonious alliance between the two realms. With an astute appreciation for scientific inquiry, he upheld that spirituality played a complementary role in grappling with existential inquiries and delving into the profound depths of the human experience. Embracing both domains is essential to understanding the world and our place.

New Inputs From Past Knowledge

Vivekananda blended religion with nationalism and applied this reinterpretation to various aspects of education and faith. He synthesised and popularised various strands of Hindu thought, most notably classical yoga and Advaita Vedanta. His beliefs were not based on blind worship but on learning that evolved over his lifetime. They were shaped by concepts like Brahmo Samaj, which included belief in a shapeless God. Similarly, Swami Ranganathananda did not confine himself to developing spiritual ideas alone but sought to bring practical applications of ancient wisdom into modern contexts. His lecture series throughout the Western hemisphere centred around this idea.

Furthermore, Swami Vivekananda and Ranganathananda promoted and emphasised the fundamental ideas of character building and co-existence within Indian society. The understanding is that although humans are social beings and live and work in society, before an individual can contribute to the reordering of society, they must first attain specific characteristics and undergo self-development. Looking back at traditional heritage to provide suggestions for the contemporary period are precisely the role of education. The notion that social evils can be fought by individuals professing spirituality may not feel congruent to many who follow Western philosophies; still, in India, spirituality has a higher essence of bringing harmony and justice to society.

While visionary agendas and advanced discussions mark India's pursuit of becoming a developed nation, IKS is a crucial yet often overlooked pillar in this journey. Recognising the wisdom of the past and integrating it into modern contexts through education and societal engagement can significantly contribute to India's development goals. Swami Vivekananda and Ranganathananda serve as exemplars of blending science with spirituality, advocating for a holistic understanding of existence. Embracing IKS preserves India's rich heritage and fosters a deeper connection with nature and society, which is essential for shaping the nation's sustainable and inclusive future.

Both Vivekananda and Ranganathananda bridged the Cartesian divide between science and religion. Speaking about this, Swami Vivekananda said, "Science is nothing but the finding of unity." It matters little what we call that state of unity, but the fact remains that the goal of all knowledge, philosophy, science, religion, and all endeavours is to find that unity. Consciously or unconsciously, we are all moving towards that grand unification. In the *Bharatiya* narrative architecture, there is no Cartesian divide, but by opting for the right balance between religion, spirituality and science, one can bring a high level of synergy t life. It is not either/or; but a balance and harmony with the entire cosmos.

33

Civilisational Connection of Ayodhya's Ram Temple

The fact that the Ram temple in Ayodhya took nearly 76 years after Independence to be built due to the uproar surrounding it, is unwarranted. The temples that were destroyed by the Islamist invaders and mosques built on their very site are never discussed, nor the lives of the crores who were massacred in the genocide of Hindus. Even today, some argue the mosque must be rebuilt; but what about the temple that was destroyed and the mosque built over it? While Abrahamic faiths have their holy cities, Hindus have been denied in the name of secularism in the name of the Nehruvian and Left variety their basic rights to have their *asmita* (pride) and *aastha* (belief) restored. For them, secularism is the preferential treatment of all except the majority of Hindus. By this definition, one is secular if one criticises Hindus and is blind to the Abrahamic faiths. If you practice real secularism, that is, criticise all, then you are branded a coward and a communal.

It is a moment of civilisational pride for every *Bharatiya* that the symbol of Ram unites diverse people across continents. Ram is the symbol of civilisation where the unity of Ram in diverse interpretations has fascinated us for several centuries. Every civilisation is proud of its symbols of pride and identity and who are these detractors to deny that, while they themselves practice all forms of false consciousnesses?

These individuals have, for decades, arrogated to themselves the right to define Hinduism as they deem fit and only as they deem fit. Two eminent distortions have the unique distinction of being among the most vocal and unrelenting voices opposing the archaeological results of the excavations in Ayodhya against the backdrop of the dispute over the land demolished at the erstwhile Babri Masjid. Another group is foreigners who do not know the classical languages but wax eloquent positions on Hinduism and Hindutva.

Their whitewashing of the temple destructions that took place under Aurangzeb's rule, their blatant misrepresentations of incidents from the Ramayana through mistranslations and other important aspects are studied through a careful analysis of their writings.

The Ram Mandir movement wasn't just a movement for any temple. It was a struggle for a temple at the Janmabhoomi of Lord Ram, India's identity. Over 3.7 lakh sacrificed their lives for this movement. This is a reassertion of the *Bharatiya* identity, a pride, an announcement that the Hindus have arrived to be treated as equals with other faiths who have always hegemonically determined what they should define as who we are. 22 January 2024 declares we are ready to say what it means to be a *Bharatiya*, and there is nothing to be ashamed of. It is a reclamation and a reminder for us, with our age-old civilisation proven scientifically beyond 8,000 years.

When the legal battle was won, it was decided that a grand and magnificent temple would be built in Ayodhya. It was also decided that the Ram temple should not be built by the government or any business person like the Laxminarayan temple had been and became more popular as the Birla temple. The larger society had fought for 500 years for the temple at Ayodhya, so it was decided that they should approach society to construct the Ram temple. It was a people's movement, a democratic struggle against hegemonic interpretations of distorted history. As a grand temple has now been constructed in Ayodhya, it will be a Ram Mandir of the crores of people who gave whatever they could. The masses have a stake in Ram Mandir, now their mandir, of connecting tradition with modernity, continuity with change, realm with region and myth with reality.

Indeed, Hindus are not dogmatic. Hindus are decentralised in that Hindu Dharma is more a family of spiritual traditions than a single path. The family of traditions that is today called Hinduism has a certain rootedness. That rootedness is evident outwardly in the Hindu's sacred geography. This culminates in specific important *kshetras* (holy places). These *kshetras*, spread throughout India, are held sacred across the country's spiritual traditions. It has created the very nation of India, and this movement is still India's civilisational life force. When this movement ceases, Bharat as a nation will cease to exist. If Bharat as a nation ceases to exist, then India as a state cannot stand for a decade. The destruction of the holy shrines in the *kshetras* of *teertha yatra* (pilgrimage) has a more devastating impact on Hindus as a nation than on the holy shrines of the so-called Abrahamic faiths. For the Abrahamic faiths, a holy site is historical. Its recovery or possession is a symbol of victory of the faith. But for Hindus, the loss of a *teertha kshetra* (pilgrimage site) is the loss of a part of their civilisational life. The Ayodhya movement, at its heart, challenged not only the Islamist destruction of the temple but also the neglect and systematic destruction in slow motion of the holy cities themselves by the Nehruvian state.

Prime Minister Narendra Modi has become the redeemer of a nation searching for its soul, which is embodied by Ram's persona. The persistence of this idea, reinforced by the imaginations of a people and a ruler who turns his every working day into a renewal of the pledge and promise of an *Amrit Kaal*, is democracy's most compelling story today. Those who are in a state of anxiety and panic will be left by the wayside. It has created the very passion of *Bharat* and this movement is still India's civilisational and national life force. Since 2014, Prime Minister Modi has been the sole spokesperson of a civilisational state in search of cultural justice, his faith in the possibilities of Bharat, where he played the moderniser and the cultural restorer consolidating all social identities into the civilisational unity represented by the image of Ram the redeemer is a masterstroke and a paradigm shift.

34

Perception Warfare Subverting Democracies and Societies

Alvin Toffler said, "The full implications of what we term 'Third wave knowledge warfare' have not yet been digested. Future wars will increasingly be prevented, won, or lost based on information superiority and dominance. Cyberwar involves everything from strategic deception and perception management to tactical disruption of an adversary's information systems."

An array of unconventional strategies focused on expanding their international influence to achieve national security objectives has been developed. They have deployed anti-access area denial platforms, coercive economic practices, deception, information operations, and utilisation of proxies. Open societies and democracies face this danger all the more. With the availability of technology, deepfakes are being created, which can spread havoc through instant social media. This is a warfare by deception. It indicates a shift towards more subtle engagement methods, conducted discreetly behind the scenes, to undermine adversaries from within. This strategy employs a 'death by a thousand cuts' philosophy, eschewing single-point actions to utilise various smaller measures across media, social platforms, political discourse, and even popular culture.

The application of these undermining actions, sometimes understood as information warfare, varies across different political systems. Autocratic regimes, with their absolute control over the media, absence of electoral processes, and readiness to resort to violent suppression methods, are better equipped to handle and restrict such undermining efforts.

Their tight grip on power leaves little room for adversaries to sow discord and chaos. Conversely, democracies, particularly those characterised by multicultural and multiethnic populations (such as India), are more susceptible to subversion. Tensions and grievances from the past can be easily manipulated and exploited, making these societies vulnerable to external interference and subversion tactics.

Misusing Technology

One critical foundation for such subversion lies in the misuse of technological tools, especially the media, including print, online, and volatile social media platforms. With its encompassing iconography, popular culture has also emerged as a potent tool. We see this in US universities like University of California, Los Angeles and Columbia University, where these tools are used to target youth, who are more susceptible to propaganda and half-baked ideas. What often ensues from such measures is the complete disregard for context and proportion, rallying people around shallow notions. Moreover, societal ignorance makes such radical and toxic ideas easier to gain ground. The obliviousness of American youth about the horrors of the Holocaust is a big reason for their support of the glamorisation of such ideas. In consequence, American youth a ironically supporting Hamas, which categorically committed the most brutal attacks against the Jewish population since the Holocaust. Meanwhile, anti-Semitism has become a daily feature of campus life in the US, the supposed land of free speech and the rule of law.

India has its share of problems in this regard, as the narrative of Hindu hatred has become prevalent in the US and many Western educational establishments, often downplayed as isolated incidents. Selective reporting, aided by ideologically motivated individuals who view India negatively, has perpetuated this narrative. Similarly, concerning Indian politics, we saw the recent deepfake video of Indian Home Minister Amit Shah go viral, with almost all major international news outlets covering it due to its incendiary content. Yet, not everyone followed up on their stories to correct the negative coverage after it was found to be fake. Intriguingly, individuals without voting rights in India are considered experts on Indian democratic traditions, which surprisingly shape and skew the narrative.

And when their incorrect prophecies are proven false, they often double down, attributing the discrepancy to some hidden agenda. Over the last decade, this pattern has repeated itself with no accountability from these journalists and media houses misusing the power of technology to do so.

Erosion of Democracy and Societal Values

The propagation of radical ideas aimed at undermining societies has become so easy and effective that the concept of protest funding is now a prominent concern in many countries. Particularly during electoral cycles, we witness protest funding becoming a flash point in election discourse in the US and India. Students who come to universities to learn are often incited with misguided and ill-informed ideas, manipulated to suit the interests of adversaries. This raises concerns about who would be willing to fight wars if the narrative and public discourse have become so fragile.

Media houses and ill-motivated civil societies must be carefully watched for these reasons. *The Washington Post* is a good example of a media giant that has shaped itself into such a force that it disseminates fabricated narratives, to which even nations like India and Israel find themselves obliged to respond. Ideally, this should not be the case. Still, when news outlets propagate half-baked information laced with ideological poison, the need to respond becomes essential. In the current context, whether it's the misfiring of a rocket by Palestinian Islamic Jihad on a hospital in Gaza or elections or COVID-19 in India, we see the ideological slant of these media houses and their obligations to espouse a particular narrative of the so-called 'death of democracy'. At the same time, outright violence within the US is wholly played down.

Countering Perception Warfare

Three major priorities come to mind that require serious attention and deliberation. First, there is a critical need for youth education, particularly in countries where the youth population is growing. Despite having more resources than previous generations, the transmission of education and wisdom from past generations has somehow faltered. Therefore, it is imperative to educate the youth about the history, culture, religions, traditions, and literature of their country and society to prevent the caricatures that enemies might seek to push within our country from gaining ground. Part of these efforts is also to cleanse the curricula of ideological biases and propaganda.

Second, technology is a potent tool for propagating both excellent and destructive ideas. It's essential to recognise that while the positive aspects are maximised, the negative ones are kept in check. This entails implementing better cyber (including AI) hygiene practices and punishing offenders who propagate misinformation. Here, media houses must be held accountable and called out fiercely and publicly for their actions.

Third, one of the best safeguards against such subversion is a robust framework composed of societal values and ethics. No adversary can harm a society or country as much as it can hurt itself. Therefore, there is no stronger support base than a solid moral foundation. In this regard, India is fortunate to have a historical legacy from which it can draw wisdom and develop its traditions of knowledge systems. India's diverse and tolerant society has endured nearly every challenge a civilisation can face. Yet, it has proudly survived due to its traditions and societal values that promote harmony over conflict.

In conclusion, let's not compartmentalise what's happening in the US as an American phenomenon. There, these protestors are called termites and have been mercilessly arrested. Let's be aware of the lethal nature of perception warfare, how narratives are built, manipulated, and propagated, and how a society devoid of boundaries, moral codes, and a sense of historical values ultimately suffers.

35

India's Rich Democratic Legacy: From Uttaramerur to Anubhava Mandapa

The recent inauguration of the new Parliament building marked a significant milestone in India's 76-year history of Independence. For the first time, Indians have constructed a Parliament that is entirely their own, free from the influence of a colonial legacy. While the older Sansad Bhawan held great historical importance in Indian politics, the new Parliament building seeks to emphasise the spirit of democracy from an Indian perspective. In doing so, it reaches back to the rich heritage of democracy that India possesses through references to Indian history, through maps and murals. The symbolic placing of the Sengol signifies this continuity with change and tradition with modernity.

As is known, India's democratic legacy extends far beyond the very origin of democracy itself. The fact is that democracy in India was not only established earlier but was also more organised and inclusive than its counterparts in the West. For instance, in Athenian democracy, two-thirds of adults, which included foreigners, enslaved people, and even women, could not participate in the legislative processes. And yet, the narrative is forwarded as if the West and democracy are coterminous. For long, India has either willingly or tacitly consented to such narratives while being unaware, ignorant, and often ashamed of its own history.

Nonetheless, this is no longer India's approach. As a country and civilisation, India is undergoing a profound transformation, where it is becoming more confident and vocal about its actions and achievements. An excellent example of this came during Prime Minister Narendra Modi's address at the 76th session of the United Nations General Assembly (UNGA), where he proudly proclaimed, "I am representing a country which has the distinction of being named as the 'Mother of Democracy.' We have had a great tradition of democracy for thousands of years." These powerful words shed light on the deep-rooted democratic traditions that have shaped India's history. In particular, the reference to 'Mother of Democracy' highlights the vibrant democratic heritage that predates many modern Western democracies. This is based on strong historical facts of the Uttaramerur inscription, which came into existence 800 years before the Magna Carta.

From ancient times to today, India has been shaped by democratic principles and institutions that have laid the foundation for its progress and inclusivity. The earliest sources of India's democratic principles and traditions were the Indus Valley Civilisation and the Sangam period. Later, the examples of *Uttaramerur* and the *Anubhava Mandapa* stand as testaments to India's rich democratic tradition, emphasising the importance of inclusive governance, participatory decision-making, and the power of dialogue. Looking into these historical examples and their implications, one uncovers the intricate tapestry of India's democratic tradition that continues to guide the nation's path forward.

India's democratic heritage can be traced back to its ancient roots, as reflected in the mentions of '*gana* (assembly)' and '*sangha* (association)' in texts like the *Mahabharata*, Panini's *Aṣṭādhyāyī*, and Buddhist scriptures. These references provide insights into the existence of republics and confederacies, illustrating the decentralised nature of governance and the active participation of the people. The Vedic era, in particular, sheds light on the democratic essence through two significant assemblies: the *samiti* and the *sabha*. These terms signify the presence of decentralised forms of governance and collaborative associations. Such historical evidence highlights the early democratic principles embedded within Indian society.

Among these references, the *Mahabharata* is the first textual source to mention a republican form of government, employing the terms *gana* and *sangha*. This indicates that the concept of self-governing bodies and collective decision-making was already prevalent. One noteworthy example of early democracy found in the *Mahabharata* is the *samiti*. It served as an experiment in direct democracy. This system continues to exist in some parts of the world today. The *samiti* operated as a platform for the active participation of citizens in decision-making processes. It played a crucial role in electing and re-electing kings, demonstrating the democratic principle of popular choice and accountability. Attendance at the *samiti* was mandatory for the king (*Rājan*), emphasising the importance of their interaction with the people.

In addition to the *samiti*, the *sabha* was another notable assembly during the Vedic era. It was closely associated with the *samiti* and was often considered its refined counterpart. The *sabha*, a 'body of men shining together', functioned as a house of elders. It was significant, as even deities and respected sages attended its sessions. The *sabha* acted as a parliamentary body for conducting debates and discussions on matters of public interest, reflecting the democratic ethos of open dialogue and deliberation. The position of *sabhapati*, the chairman of the *sabha*, was held in high esteem. The modern-day Upper House of Parliament (Rajya Sabha) is widely considered a successor to the *sabha*. Consequently, the *samiti* represents the modern-day Lok Sabha or the Lower House of Parliament.

Basically, these ancient democratic institutions demonstrate the early recognition of participatory governance in India. They showcase the active involvement of citizens in decision-making processes, the significance of collective wisdom, and the value placed on eloquence and debating skills. Such assemblies reveal the deep-rooted democratic traditions that have shaped India's political history. The *samiti*, resembling a legislature, convened to discuss state matters and elect or re-elect kings. It emphasised the importance of a true king attending the assembly, signifying accountability to the people. The *sabha*, a body of elders, conducted public business through debate and discussion, reflecting the values of free expression and collective decision-making. In other words, these early democratic institutions paved the way for inclusive governance and highlighted the significance of open dialogue and participation.

Within the vast tapestry of India's democratic heritage, the Anubhava Mandapa and the Uttaramerur inscriptions stand out as significant examples. The Anubhava Mandapa was founded by the visionary social reformer Basavanna in Karnataka during the 12th century and, thus, holds great significance in India's history. This institution can be seen as an early version of a parliament, where mystics, saints, and philosophers assembled to discuss various topics encompassing society, economy, culture, and spirituality. Basavanna's foresight led to establishing this public forum a century before the famous Magna Carta emerged in England. Situated in Basavakalyan, Karnataka's Bidar district, the Anubhava Mandapa played a pivotal role in fostering an egalitarian renaissance, thereby serving as the genesis of parliamentary democracy in India. Scholars, poets, and philosophers congregated at this place to exchange knowledge and insights, cultivating an atmosphere of inclusivity and progressive thinking. This tradition exemplifies the deeply ingrained democratic values within India's cultural and intellectual heritage. By embracing the lessons from these ancient democratic institutions, India can strengthen its dedication to inclusivity, ensuring that every voice is acknowledged and represented.

Another is the case of Uttaramerur, a historical village in Tamil Nadu that provides a remarkable example of a well-organised democratic structure that thrived in ancient India. Established in 750 CE, it boasted of a vibrant democratic system with temples, wards, dependent hamlets, tanks, and roads. Meticulous planning and inclusivity were the cornerstones of Uttaramerur's electoral system, ensuring that only eligible individuals who met specific qualifications could contest elections.

The village consisted of 30 wards, and during elections, the entire community, including infants, would gather at the village assembly *mandapa*. Committees maintained irrigation tanks and roads and provided relief during droughts. Uttaramerur's elective system showcased meticulous planning and inclusivity. Its constitution defined qualifications for candidates, ensuring that only eligible individuals above 35 years and below 70, who owned taxable land and a legally owned house, could contest elections.

Inscriptions found in Uttaramerur provide valuable insights into this efficient system of governance. More than 200 inscriptions discovered in the village shed light on its self-governance abilities and the sophistication of its local population. The system discouraged corruption and wrongdoing, as elected members who engaged in such practices faced disqualification. Furthermore, committee members were ineligible for re-election for the subsequent three terms. The inscriptions found in Uttaramerur shed light on its self-governance abilities, revealing a system that discouraged corruption and provided checks and balances. As such, Prime Minister Narendra Modi's references to the Anubhava Mandapa and the Uttaramerur inscriptions underscore India's democratic heritage that as he correctly pointed out, predates the Magna Carta. These examples demonstrate the deeply embedded nature of democratic traditions within India's social fabric long before their formal establishment in the modern era.

For such profound reasons, India's democratic legacy holds invaluable lessons that can shape the nation's future. Upholding the principles of inclusivity, accountability, and participatory governance is vital to safeguard the nation's essence. Moving ahead, India must firmly cherish its democratic values and nurture the seeds of democracy sown by its ancestors. By drawing inspiration from its illustrious past, India can serve as a guiding light for democratic ideals, leading the way in promoting equality, justice, and prosperity for all its citizens. The preservation and celebration of India's democratic heritage will pave the path for a brighter future for generations to come.

While reflecting on India's rich democratic legacy, one must also remember the words of former Prime Minister Atal Bihari Vajpayee: "Governments will come and go, political parties will emerge and fade away. However, India should remain; its democracy should remain immortal." Upholding the democratic principles derived from ancient experiences is essential to protect the nation's soul.

In conclusion, the *Anubhava Mandapa* and the *Uttaramerur* inscriptions are remarkable testaments to India's thriving democratic traditions since ancient times. They illuminate the presence of well-structured institutions and inclusive electoral systems that predate Western notions of modern democracy. As India progresses, it must draw inspiration from its illustrious past and deeply cherish its democratic values, ensuring they continue to shape the nation for generations to come. It is a paradigm shift that we are not only stating, accepting and building an alternative narrative, but also challenging the hegemonic Western narrative of superiority and civilising mission that were constructed on a false consciousness.

Foreign Policy

36

Kachchatheevu and the Debate on Geo-economics and Maritime Security

India is often seen and described as a subcontinent and not a peninsula because of its vast lands, which blur its ocean frontiers. The peninsular character of India and its dependence on maritime traffic give the sea a dominant influence on its destiny. However, a one-sided view of India's security, with an exclusive focus on north-west frontiers overlooked the oceanic environment and its advantages and disadvantages. Sardar KM Panikkar had the vision to understand peninsular India's oceanic navigation legacy and wrote extensively for Indian policymakers.

Possession of islands away from the mainland provides strategic and political advantages to a country. The security and preservation of island territories from state and non-state actors is vital. It is like a game of 'chess'. All major world powers compete to show their presence militarily, diplomatically, and politically to gain a foothold in the Indian Ocean Region. The region has become a theatre for conflict against Chinese domination, which has led to the Quad, composed of democratic forces. If only India had used its maritime power as envisaged by Panikkar, the Indian Ocean would have become an Indian lake.

Recently, a controversy has emerged surrounding the uninhabited islet of Kachchatheevu which spans 1.9 square kilometres in the Palk Strait and is located approximately 14 nautical miles off Rameswaram in India. Despite previously existing in relative obscurity, this issue has garnered national attention following Prime Minister Narendra Modi's tweet, which thrust it into the spotlight. Yet, the increased focus has not been commensurate with a proportional increase in awareness or understanding of the controversy.

Diplomacy that Overlooked Democracy

The core of the dispute surrounding Kachchatheevu revolves around competing sovereignty claims, with Sri Lanka asserting historical rights dating back to the Portuguese occupation (1505 to1658 CE). In contrast, India maintains that the erstwhile Raja of Ramnad (Ramanathapuram) had possession of the islet as part of his *zamindari* (land ownership system), with taxes collected until 1947 when the government took it over. The Nehru government's initial neglect and trivialisation of the issue's importance, particularly its impact on the fisherfolk community, was concerning. In June 1974, an agreement was signed between the Indira Gandhi government and the Sri Lankan counterpart, RD Bandaranaike, granting fishermen from both countries the right to fish around the islet.

Subsequently, a follow-up agreement in March 1976 clarified that fishing vessels and fishermen from either country were prohibited from engaging in fishing activities in specific maritime zones without express permission from Sri Lanka or India. The agreements, the government reasoned, were made to maintain amicable relations with Sri Lanka. However, what was problematic from the Indian viewpoint was the decision to recognise Sri Lankan sovereignty over Kachchatheevu, which was made by the government without the proper involvement of Parliament, sparking significant opposition across political parties. Although the matter in India remains sub judice, the point remains that diplomacy overlooked the democratic process.

Accountability in Foreign Policy

The presumption that negotiations or compromises in diplomacy are made through cold calculation, as argued for the 1974/76 agreements, overlooks the crucial role of due diligence in decision-making processes. While negotiations may appear calculated, they must be based on thorough research and analysis, of which the evidence contradicts. Moreover, the involvement of domestic politics, particularly the role of the Dravida Munnetra Kazhagam, highlights how internal dynamics can significantly influence the foreign policy decisions of the Union government.

While seeking peaceful resolutions to boundary disputes is a fundamental diplomatic challenge for modern Westphalian states, it should not precede due diligence, accountability, and competence. For such reasons, the current dispensation stands out for its awareness of its power and weaknesses within the international system and, therefore, has adopted an increasingly assertive position that balances realism with idealism. This contrasts with the handling of the Kachchatheevu issue, which illustrated incompetence, arrogance, and unaccountability.

India has maintained amicable relations with its neighbours, including Sri Lanka. However, when signing agreements, it is essential to consider the country's and its people's long-term interests. From Sri Lanka's perspective in 1974, asserting sovereignty over Kachchatheevu was in their national interest. The question arises: Where was India's long-term perspective in giving away its territory, and why was it done secretly?

Necessity of Democratic Process and Maritime Security

The Kachchatheevu controversy is a reminder of the vital role that democracy and the political process play in discussions on foreign policy matters. In navigating complex foreign policy decisions, making cold, rational choices can be challenging and may necessitate hard choices. However, as long as these decisions are reached through consensus and transparency, there is a firm belief that the public will stand behind their government.

Meanwhile, the revelation of Kachchatheevu also presents a silver lining, highlighting two crucial trends in Indian politics. Firstly, it underscores the importance of checks and balances within the political system, allowing such matters to be brought to light, debated, and to raise awareness among the public. Secondly, this revelation occurred during an electoral process, where the focus is traditionally on ad hominem attacks, which signifies a positive shift towards policy-centred discussions and debates. It reflects a growing trend where the public is increasingly interested in understanding policy issues and making informed choices.

Geo-Economics and Maritime Security

While matters related to infrastructure or the economy may command immediate attention due to their direct impact on the public, foreign policy and defence issues are equally significant, albeit their effects may manifest over time. The Sagarmala Project, approved in 2015, harnesses the 7,500 km long coastline for economic development. The project also seeks to boost infrastructure for transporting goods to and from ports quickly, efficiently, and cost-effectively. Here, islands like Kachchatheevu have become very strategic.

India has enjoyed positive relations with Sri Lanka, and that ensuring these revelations do not strain ties is imperative. However, the episode underscores the necessity for truth, transparency, and public participation in navigating the complexities and challenges inherent in foreign policy matters. Framed in this context, the Kachchatheevu issue is about the broader debates on diplomacy and democracy in India, where the goal must be the preservation of truth and the integrity of democratic and political processes. No wonder India brought maritime security to the UN Security Council, and Prime Minister Narendra Modi chaired it. He called for a roadmap for maritime security cooperation based on the principles of cooperation he outlined. This is the kind of initiative that Sardar KM Panikkar had envisaged many decades ago.

37

A New Kind of Terrorism: Savvier, Yet Deadlier

The recent appalling terrorist attacks in Russia, claiming the lives of at least 137 individuals, serve as a grim reminder of the most pressing challenge facing modern nation-states: terrorism carried out by armed non-state actors driven by ideologies and religious fanaticism. One suspects the involvement of several actors due to the strategic and military sophistication of the attack. Why would Islamic terrorist groups attack Russia in the post-Hamas-Israel war scenario? These questions remain, and Russian suspicions are directed Ukraine and its proxies in this grey and hybrid warfare.

Contemporary terrorism is unique not merely for its modus operandi but rather for the alarming expansion of its reach, the ease with which attacks are orchestrated, and the sophistication exhibited by the perpetrators. As such, this evolving landscape of terror demands a comprehensive reassessment of counter-terrorism strategies that acknowledges these violent actors' evolving tactics and capabilities.

Unlike earlier endeavours driven primarily by strategic objectives or the need to establish international networks as a means of evading domestic crackdowns, today's terrorists are increasingly motivated by grim theatrics of carnage. As we grapple with this evolving form of terrorism unfolding on a global scale, three key considerations demand our attention:

An Edge over Intelligence Agencies?

The escalating challenge of terrorist attacks in recent years poses a critical dilemma for intelligence agencies worldwide: maintaining an edge over adversaries who exploit vulnerabilities with alarming precision. By their very mandate, intelligence agencies operate pre-emptively, recognising that post-event responses offer scant recourse. They collect, analyse, and disseminate information to decision-makers, which is crucial for safeguarding national security interests.

Intelligence can be broadly categorised into two vital streams: strategic and operational intelligence. The former encompasses data for formulating long-term national security strategies, often entwined with geopolitical dynamics and power competition among states. However, the lion's share of intelligence work falls under the operational domain, where time-sensitive information must be swiftly deployed. Failure to act promptly renders such intelligence obsolete because it carries grave and immediate consequences.

As technological advancements increasingly shape the landscape of intelligence gathering, there has been a concerning shift away from human intelligence towards Signal Intelligence. This over-reliance on technology has inadvertently provided the terrorists with opportunities to manipulate information, blurring the line between actionable intelligence and misinformation. The consequence is a disturbing trend of large-scale and lethal terrorist attacks persisting across the globe. Meanwhile, despite advancements in their capacities and increased security measures, states find it challenging to keep up.

Changing the Profile of Terrorists

The profile of terrorists is undergoing a profound shift. Gone are the days when terrorists were stereotyped as illiterate, poor, cave-dwelling individuals with a lack of technological savvy and linguistic skills. In the contemporary landscape, terrorists represent a new breed: educated, tech-savvy, multilingual, and often blending seamlessly into society until apprehended.

The recent arrests in India serve as a stark reminder of this evolving threat. Among those apprehended were individuals with impressive educational backgrounds, including a student of biotechnology at IIT Guwahati who had allegedly sworn allegiance to ISIS. This underscores the unsettling reality that modern terrorists are drawn from diverse backgrounds, often defying conventional stereotypes and, therefore, more difficult to apprehend and their terror attacks more challenging to avoid.

Yet, it is crucial to maintain perspective when discussing the phenomenon of foreign fighters and mercenaries joining ISIS from India. While a notable number have been identified, it pales compared to the influx from Europe and the US, despite much smaller populations. This underscores the complex interplay of factors influencing terrorist recruitment and highlights the success of Indian intelligence agencies that were able to apprehend and break the terrorist rings recruiting for ISIS.

Terrorism through Information Warfare

As noted, in the current era of terrorism, there is an emergence of highly tech-savvy individuals who have grown up in the digital age. These modern terrorists are adept at leveraging technological tools, leading to the rise of information warfare tactics aimed at either crafting elaborate conspiracies or undermining legitimate efforts. A striking example can be observed in the case of Israel's conflict in Gaza, where narratives have swiftly shifted against Israel, even preceding the involvement of the Israel Defence Forces (IDF). This manipulation of information in cyberspace poses a formidable challenge for intelligence agencies, impeding their ability to respond swiftly and effectively.

In addition to the proliferation of tech-savvy terrorists, social media has emerged as a potent tool for radicalisation, particularly among young individuals. Issues unfolding in one corner of the globe can swiftly ignite anger and fear, and even spur action in distant lands. While the world caught a glimpse of this phenomenon during the Yugoslav crises in the 1990s, the present reality is marked by instant incitement platforms such as Instagram and Facebook, where ill-intentioned individuals amplify and disseminate manipulated information with alarming speed.

The manipulation of information on these platforms has the potential to stoke violent reactions in various countries, irrespective of whether the underlying tensions are religious or ethnic. Terrorism, regardless of its guise, must be unequivocally condemned and combated. However, the battleground is evolving, with cyberspace increasingly becoming a primary arena for extremist activities.

As the lines between physical and cyber warfare blur, addressing the complexities of modern terrorism demands a multifaceted approach. It necessitates enhanced technological capabilities to counter online radicalization and robust international cooperation to tackle the global dissemination of extremist ideologies. India has emerged as a driver of the global counter-terrorism agenda, but when it comes to domestic efforts to keep up with evolving terrorism, there is a need to redirect more focus towards developing a new generation of individuals, who can keep up with the changing threat of terrorism.

A clear case is the involvement of Canada in harbouring Khalistani terrorists on their soil to attack another sovereign democratic state Is the spillover of competitive domestic politics ruining a sane and impartial foreign policy? Technology is a double-edged weapon. In both the recent attacks in Israel and Russia, the involvement of the Islamist group named alone, without proxies is questioned. The reason is the level of sophistication, and the machinery used is beyond the capabilities of these groups. Hence, the needle of suspicion moves beyond the involvement of those who possess this technology as part of grey or hybrid warfare.

38

Sudan's Human Rights Crisis and an Exercise in Global Hypocrisy

The intellectual class often takes pride in their commitment to humanity, frequently emphasizing their advocacy for human rights. However, this commitment remains selective, myopic, and politically influenced. For instance, Hamas' brutal attacks on civilians, including children, women, and the elderly, failed to elicit their concern. Only when Israel responded to what is considered the most severe attack against the Jewish population since the Holocaust did human rights become a focal point. The same thing happened with the humanitarian crisis involving Afghans in Pakistan. These individuals faced atrocious and inhumane expulsion by Pakistan. Yet, the intellectual class' response to this crisis has been noticeably muted. This raises questions about the genuine commitment to humanity and whether such concerns are driven by political motivations rather than an unwavering dedication to human rights. But can these two be isolated examples? Let's take another case of Sudan.

Africa has been a neglected continent despite its rich heritage and natural resources. It has faced the worst effects of colonialism and genocide, and now we are watching like mute audiences the replay of another such genocide. In the recently concluded G20 under India's Presidency, Prime Minister Narendra Modi took the courageous step of including the African Union as a G20 + 1 member at the New Delhi summit. This was indeed once again informing the international community of the voice of the Global South, especially Africa. Sudan is grappling with a severe humanitarian crisis and one of the worst human rights situations in its history. The Human Rights Watch's

World Report 2023 presents a sombre depiction of widespread abuses and attacks against civilians, in Darfur, compounded by the lingering aftermath of the October 2021 coup. To comprehend the gravity of the situation, one must consider the humanitarian crisis detailed by the UN Office for the Coordination of Humanitarian Affairs. In 2023, a staggering eight million people in Sudan will require assistance, with seven million internally displaced individuals, including over 350,000 displaced in 2022. The funding shortfall, currently standing at US$ 862 million out of the required US$ 1.9 billion, starkly underscores the inadequacy of the international response to address the urgent needs of the Sudanese people.

A majority Muslim country, Sudan is entangled in a complex web of ethnic and religious tensions that have persisted for decades. The current struggles the nation faces are not solely a contemporary crisis but rather a legacy of past conflicts that have left an indelible mark on its landscape. The enduring repercussions of conflicts in Darfur, South Kordofan, and Blue Nile, as well as the scars of the civil war in South Sudan, contribute to the simmering tensions.

In addition to the militia violence that has escalated over the past two years, existing government institutions are proving inadequate in delivering justice. Individuals are subjected to ill-treatment within judicial proceedings, underscoring the alarming nature of the human rights crisis in Sudan. This crisis demands urgent attention; yet the global response has been insufficient, clouded by political considerations and diplomatic manoeuvring. The plight of the Sudanese people, particularly the violation of religious freedom and the erosion of justice, calls for a more concerted and principled international effort to address the unfolding human rights tragedy. Compounding the suffering, outbreaks of malaria, hepatitis, measles, and dengue fever in 2022 have further burdened a population already grappling with the consequences of conflict and political instability.

It is disheartening to acknowledge that, often, human rights violations only seem to capture attention when they pertain to a specific religion. This trend is, once again, observable in the case of Sudan. Earlier, in 2019, the removal of President Omar al-Bashir sparked optimism for an end to the persecution of Christians in Sudan, as the transitional government committed to abolishing discriminatory laws. However, since the 2021 coup, a distressing reality has unfolded, marked by the attack and confiscation of church properties, harassment, and detention of leaders. The once-promised religious freedom has crumbled under the weight of political turmoil.

Yet, amidst these dire circumstances, a pertinent question arises: will this grave situation awaken the conscience of intellectuals and the global community to protect the vulnerable? The enormity of the crisis demands a collective and conscientious response to alleviate the profound suffering experienced by the Sudanese population.

The trend among self-proclaimed intellectuals in India is to incessantly question and critique India's responses through their news articles. The Palestinian issue has dominated recent parliamentary and public discourse, subjecting the Ministry of External Affairs (MEA) responses to microscopic examination. Doubts are cast on the human nature of India's policy and its commitment to the Palestinian cause, with questions raised about whether India has abandoned Palestine. Strikingly absent from their discussions is any notable concern or awareness about Sudan, except when they wish to criticise the handling of the crisis by the MEA. Also missing are the marches or extensive opinion pieces one might expect in the face of such a grave crisis. Instead, the discourse is relegated to smaller pieces on the margins of editorials, often questioning India's perceived inadequate response.

It is worth mentioning that such an indifferent and, in some cases, ignorant attitude demeans India's proactive actions. The successful Operation Kaveri, which saw the evacuation of over 3,000 Indians from Sudan, received little attention. A case in point is India's recent hosting of the G20 summit. In this rare opportunity to host the event, India actively collaborated with the Global South, advocating for the inclusion of the African Union as a G20 member. However, those viewing the world through ideological lenses dismiss these accomplishments as irrelevant and inadequate.

Ultimately, the glaring hypocrisy surrounding human rights violations in Sudan highlights the selective attention and subdued responses of the intellectuals. When the discourse on human rights is swayed by political expediency rather than an unwavering commitment to justice, the very essence of the term is compromised. It is incumbent upon the global community to confront this hypocrisy and translate rhetoric into meaningful action to alleviate the profound suffering of the Sudanese people. Unfortunately, this disparity is particularly notable in India, where the intellectual class, often quick to criticise the government and institutions for human rights violations, appears indifferent to the plight of Sudan. Essentially, this underscores the need for readers to approach discussions on human rights with caution, as they may often be characterised by selectivity and lack of objectivity. The imperative lies in fostering a more just and compassionate world where humanity takes precedence over political considerations.

39

Terrorism as Business and Some NGOs as Fronts

> "All animals are equal, but some animals are more equal than others. The creatures outside looked from pig to man, and from man to pig, and from pig to man again; but already it was impossible to say which was which. Man is the only creature that consumes without producing."
>
> – George Orwell, in *Animal Farm*

Hamas leaders, who live and travel in luxury, are not affected by the global uproar over the events of 7 October. The wealth of the top leadership of Hamas is astounding; politics is no longer the last resort of the scoundrel but rather a non-state actor that doubles up as a social service organisation and a terror outfit. They work behind the façade of schools, hospitals, even refugee camps and in heavily crowded city centres. It is a typical Dr. Jekyll and Mr. Hyde situation where by day they are doing social services and by night, all criminal activities like drug trafficking, terrorism, looting, plundering, and rape. They legitimise these by doublespeak regarding their own faith, where suicide is haram; but they interpret and glorify suicide bombing as divinely ordained.

How can one separate combatants from civilians? The façade of these cowards is civilian, especially women and children. When they kill their own, no one speaks, but when others kill them, there is an uproar. This global hypocrisy of human rights and its selective uproar has numbed the honest and genuine global conscience. Are we heading to a Dystopia where fraud is the reality, killing by one is victimhood, and when the other retaliates, it becomes genocide? Victimhood has been perfected even when they are not the real victims; victims do not elect terror outfits to rule over them and legitimise their activities.

The consequences of money laundering, terror financing, and proliferation financing (providing funds or financial services for nuclear, chemical, or biological weapons), but related crimes, undermine the financial sector and the broader economy. These crimes can make countries less stable, weakening law and order and governance, undermining regulatory effectiveness, reducing foreign investments, and blocking international capital flows. Money laundering and terror financing in one country can have serious ripple effects across borders and even globally. Countries with weak or ineffective controls are attractive to money launderers and financiers of terrorism. These criminals seek to conceal their criminal activities by exploiting the complexity of the global financial system, differences between national laws, and the speed at which money can cross borders.

There are five crucial components of terrorism: the involvement of a violent act, an audience, the creation of a mood of fear, innocent victims, and political goals or motives. David C. Rapoport's 2004 essay, 'The Four Waves of Modern Terrorism', is one of the most influential and widely debated theories in the field of terrorism studies. In his essay, Professor Rapoport outlines a wave system that maps the history of modern terrorism since the late 19th century; more importantly for our purposes, it attempts to take the complex phenomenon of terrorism and put it in a historical context that not only explained different periods of international terrorism but also sets forth theories and concepts that may be used to attempt to anticipate the future of terrorism. A new fifth wave will emerge and take over in the next decade, and these alternative futures will pose ethical challenges for lawmakers and policy officials in balancing public safety and freedom.

The New Left wave started to ebb during the 1980s with the end of the Cold War. The effectiveness of participating terrorist groups was weakened by their inability to negotiate conflicting demands imposed by various international elements operating together. Navigating the competing needs of different groups resulted in the neglect of their domestic bases. The coming together of the Left Wokes with the Islamists and *jihadi* (who supports struggle) terrorists is that they follow similar tactics: fundamentally, both have deviated from their foundational principles.

The religious wave was precipitated by three major events in the Islamic world. The Iranian Revolution, the beginning of a new Islamic century, and the Soviet Union's invasion of Afghanistan all of which paved the way for religious fundamentalism to gain momentum and eclipse secular and political beliefs that motivated previous waves. In 1979, after almost two years of civil unrest and demonstrations, the Iranian Revolution unfolded, culminating in the overthrow and exile of the Shah, replacing a secular state with an Islamic Republic. The new Ayatollah regime encouraged ways to export the revolution and inspired terrorist activity in neighbouring states with large Muslim populations, including Iraq, Lebanon, Kuwait, and Saudi Arabia. To outside observers, the Iranian Revolution was unexpected, but many Muslims believed the 1979 revolution would hold significant meaning for them as it marked the start of a new Islamic century. They believed a 'redeemer' would appear, a tradition that 'sparked uprisings at the turn of earlier Muslim centuries'. Militant Islamists stormed the Grand Mosque in Mecca at the start of the new year, protesting the Saudi government, which they believed had abandoned Islamic principles.

Violent militant Islamist groups are at the heart of the religious wave and have conducted the most significant and deadly international attacks since the 1990s, but they are not the only religious terrorist organisations using violence to achieve their goals. Groups like Boko Haram, Hamas, Al Qaeda and its affiliates, Hezbollah, and ISIS have received the most international attention since the start of the religious wave.

The deep emotional resonance created by extreme religious ideology, coupled with advances in technology and other effects of globalisation, have made the religious wave of terrorism the most durable and difficult to contain. Rapoport warns that the wave pattern is so interesting and frightening that issues emerge unexpectedly to inspire terrorism, and there is no way to predict what they may be. Religious conflict involves the will of a higher power that is non-negotiable, and states cannot satisfy the demands of religiously motivated terrorists on a mission to carry out the 'Word of God'. *Jihadi* terror inspires genocidal violence to separate from the modern world, and the destruction of

Western influences—including Marxism and all its varieties—is necessary to achieve their prime objective of establishing a Caliphate.

Technology and its knowledge and use are central to the *Jihadi* terror—very much like the Left and Wokes, they talk of equality, but some are more equal, especially the Woke leadership who live in extreme luxury, which many democratic leaders cannot even dream of. It involves successful cyber-terrorism attacks intending to sabotage critical infrastructure, disrupt governments and businesses, and manipulate international financial systems. Attacks in cyberspace may be carried out by a lone wolf, acting independently or as formal groups operating under the direction of their leadership. The next generation of terrorists has grown up in a digital world, and their technical knowledge related to hacking is greater than their predecessors. They know how to penetrate sophisticated systems and bypass computer security defences, allowing them to safely and anonymously launch attacks from anywhere worldwide, while quickly adjusting their tactics in response to counter-terrorism and enhanced security measures.

Terrorists motivated by religion view their mission as a holy directive, making their goals irrefutable and non-negotiable. All major world religions have extremists that have used violence to further their perceived religious goals, but Islamist terrorist organisations have been the most active and are currently the greatest threat; some of their leaders are the neo-rich and have turned NGOs and terror into businesses to make money by violence while instilling fears among the masses.

40

Silence of the Liberals on Pakistan's Expulsion of the Afghans

In October, Pakistan's Interior Ministry delivered a severe ultimatum to around 1.7 million Afghan refugees, setting a 28-day deadline for voluntary departure or deportation. The deadline of 1 November has now elapsed, marking the commencement of mass deportations. This has been accompanied by a distressing escalation in police misconduct and brutality against Afghan migrants, exacerbating an already worsening humanitarian crisis. Shockingly, reports emerged that, in numerous cases, Afghan refugees find themselves compelled to pay hefty bribes ranging from 10,000 to 40,000 Pakistani rupees (US$ 36 to US$ 144) to escape unwarranted incarceration by Pakistani authorities.

Earlier, the aftermath of the Taliban's takeover saw an influx of Afghans into neighbouring Pakistan in 2021, spurred by government encouragement to apply for resettlement programs in countries such as the US, UK, Canada, and Germany. However, the majority of Afghans find themselves stranded with expired Pakistani visas, entangled in prolonged resettlement processes, rendering them susceptible to detention and deportation. The Taliban, on the other hand, is unlikely to take kindly to those who left the country, and many returnees would face persecution. The unfolding situation demands urgent attention to safeguard the rights and well-being of vulnerable Afghan migrants caught in the crosscurrents of geopolitical transitions.

Most striking about this humanitarian crisis is the resounding silence of the liberal community in India and abroad. Notably absent are those opportunists who previously employed liberal and moral arguments to criticise and vilify India when it enacted the CAA/National Register of Citizens (NRC) legislation through legal parliamentary means. The legislation was grounded in humanitarian concerns for persecuted religious minorities in India's neighbourhood. The stark contrast between their vocal opposition then and their current silence on a genuine humanitarian issue raises questions about the consistency and authenticity of their advocacy for human rights and liberal values. As such, three overarching aspects demand our attention.

First, the double standards of a state known best for promoting terrorism are on full display alongside the grave costs associated with sponsoring terrorism. Pakistan's rationale for expelling Afghan refugees hinges on the purported link between their presence and an upsurge in terrorist attacks, citing that 14 out of 24 bombings in the country were linked to Afghan nationals. This explanation, while ostensibly addressing security concerns, ironically underscores Pakistan's historical complicity in fostering terrorism. The proverb, "For all who take the sword will perish by the sword", resonates vividly and fittingly with Pakistan's history of sponsoring terrorism.

Second, the incident starkly showcases the double-speak of the West, including its so-called free media, which went to great lengths to criticise Indian citizenship laws. Where do organisations, self-proclaimed paragons of virtue like Amnesty International and Human Rights Watch, stand in the face of apparent hypocrisy? How much coverage is this (one of the most disastrous) crisis for the Afghan population getting worldwide? The response to the Afghan crisis so far has been conspicuously limited, focusing on highlighting the plight of Afghans without explicitly condemning the actions of the Pakistani government. This stands in stark contrast to their swift condemnation of India for enacting a legal law in Parliament, which, rather than expelling anyone, offered expedited citizenship to religiously vulnerable groups. The irony is palpable—aren't the Afghans fleeing Pakistan predominantly Muslims?

Another under-discussed hypocrisy lies in the nuanced descriptions favoured by Western critics when justifying the actions they defend. In India's case, these nuances were dismissed as excuses, but for Pakistan, they are resurrected. The United Nations Human Rights Council defended Pakistan by asserting that the Pakistani government has assured those with refugee cards will not be expelled. However, the government said that in the first wave, refugees without cards are asked to leave, suggesting that in subsequent waves, even cardholders would be expelled. Disturbingly, reports detailing harassment and expulsion threats have emerged against the cardholders, which lack the same widespread coverage afforded to Indian laws.

Third, most notably, the conspicuous silence of the Wokes, liberals, the Muslims within India, who once marched with megaphones during the NRC/CAA events, is arresting. Their silence and ignorance transcend mere overlooking of the crises; it exposes their false narrative about caring for the Muslim populace for whom they were so frantically worried. But as it turns out, their double standards are not an isolated occurrence. They cherished the Turkish criticism of Israel and support for Palestine as daring resistance. Yet, the ongoing Turkish atrocities against Kurds, primarily Muslim, are conveniently overlooked.

These self-appointed preachers of humanity reveal themselves to be nothing more than opportunistic actors with a blatant agenda—voicing and promoting their ideological biases against India. In a crude assessment, they appear to be driven by a singular goal: to undermine and denigrate India's progress, prosperity, and security. It's almost as if anything contributing to India's success irks them, compelling them to persist in their ideological crusade to defame, denounce, and deteriorate India's achievements. Their actions seem more rooted in personal animosity than in genuine concern for the principles they claim to uphold. Also, recall the reactions of these usual suspects when a viral image of the Pakistani intelligence chief in Kabul, shortly after the Taliban's takeover stirred waves of speculation and admiration within India, painting it as a display of Pakistan's adept intelligence and superior geopolitical manoeuvring. However, as events unfold, the question arises: where are those individuals now? Clearly, the Afghan crisis is not worth their time.

In essence, the complex dynamics surrounding the expulsion of Afghan refugees by Pakistan reveal that for liberals, Wokes, and the many Muslims morality is selective, the sense of caring for Muslim lives is selective, and even outrage over humanitarian crises is selective. The current situation, marked by double standards, selective Western criticism, and the telling silence within India, signals a profound crisis in public intellectual discourse. To address this, a push for increased knowledge and understanding, free from ideological biases, is imperative. Wrongdoings must be called out, while measures like CAA/NRC, aimed at safeguarding the vulnerable, deserve objective scrutiny. Dealing with the current humanitarian crises demands a genuine commitment to principles and a sincere examination of the issues at hand rather than relying on armchair critics masquerading under the pretence of humanity.

41

Terrorism as a Banality of Radical Evil

The banality of evil, initially used by Hannah Arendt to describe Nazism and Fascism seems to fit well for the present crisis inflicted by Hamas terrorists on 7 October 2023 against the state of Israel and its people. The characteristics she brought out fits so well for *Jihadi* terror. The inhumanity is glaring, and the silent majority for whom they claim to fight for don't have any say, as they don't live in a democracy in Gaza ruled by Hamas. Those far away, culturally identify with the Hamas. The enemy then and now, is the Jews. Truth is to be found in killing and dying for a fairy tale that claims to replace history. We need to see the terrifying similarities between Nazism and *Jihadi* terrorism. Hence all people need to wake up and support those fighting against this terrorist peril and not be apologetic for it. If we don't learn from history, we are condemned to repeat it. One needs to remember the words of Martin Niemöller (1892 to 1984) a prominent Lutheran pastor in Germany, "Then they came for the Jews, and I did not speak out—because I was not a Jew. Then they came for me—and there was no one left to speak for me."

October 7, 2023 freezes all humanity and the civilised world order. This is the worst killing of Jews since the Holocaust unleashed by Adolf Hitler and the National Socialist Party. The terrorist organisations complicit in this crime refuse to accept democracy, difference, diversity, dissent, and deliberations. It is necessary for us to see through this *Jihadi* terrorism, that wants only its way and rule by its fascist policies of uniformity.

Drawing on audiotapes of interviews with Eichmann by the Nazi journalist William Sassen, Stangneth presents Eichmann as a self-avowed, aggressive Nazi ideologue strongly committed to Nazi beliefs, who showed no remorse or guilt for his role in the Final Solution—a radically evil operative of the Third Reich living inside the deceptively normal shell of a bland bureaucrat. Far from being 'thoughtless', Eichmann had plenty of thoughts—thoughts of genocide, carried out on behalf of his beloved Nazi Party. On tape Eichmann admitted to a sort of Jekyll-and-Hyde dualism. In *The Origins of Totalitarianism* (1951), published well before the Eichmann trial, Arendt said: "It is inherent in our entire [Western] philosophical tradition that we cannot conceive of a 'radical evil'... One saw it unleashed then and now."

Instead of using the Eichmann case as a way forward to advance the tradition's understanding of radical evil, Arendt decided that his evil was banal, that is, 'thought defying'. By taking a narrow legalistic, formalistic approach to the trial, she emphasised that there were no deeper issues at stake beyond the legal facts of Eichmann's guilt or innocence—Arendt automatically set herself up for failure as to the deeper why of Eichmann's evil. The death cult of *Jihadi* terrorism is legitimised by the power of denial, the faith of exclusion. In 'The Origins of Totalitarianism', she argued that the evil of the Nazis was absolute and inhuman, not shallow and incomprehensible, the metaphorical embodiment of hell itself: "[T]he reality of concentration camps resembles nothing so much as medieval pictures of Hell", the ideologically evil warrior. How Eichmann's humdrum life could co-exist with that 'other' monstrous evil puzzled her. Thought defying, his genocidal acts were not. In the final analysis, Arendt did see the true horror of Eichmann's evil. In Eichmann in Jerusalem, Arendt claimed that there is a 'strange interdependence of thoughtlessness and evil', and that Eichmann's testimony had revealed the 'banality of evil'.

Both Islamic *Jihad* (Struggle) and Hamas are terrorist groups operating in Gaza that are united in their resistance against Israel and extermination of Jews. Both are also funded by and have close ties to Iran, though they function independently, Khaled Meshaal designated Friday, October 13, as the 'Day of *Jihad*', asking Muslims to take to the streets and deliver a message of anger in support of Palestinians. Is Hamas the legal and official spokesperson for the Palestinians? It is important to understand the contemporary usage of the word *Jihad*. Scholar Olivier Roy considers Syed Ahmad to be the first modern Islamic leader to lead a movement that was 'religious, military, and political' and to address the common people and rulers with a call for *jihad*. Syed Ahmad is widely regarded as the founder of the subcontinental Ahl-i Hadith movement and his teachings are highly influential among its members. Another major group that carries his legacy is the Deobandi school of thought. Scholar Edward Mortimer believes Syed Ahmad anticipated modern Islamists in waging *jihad* and attempting to create an Islamic state with strict enforcement of Sharia. Syed Ahmad attained the exemplar status of shahid (martyr), one of the highest honours in Islam, and would inspire generations of militant Islamist ideologues and *jihadi* activists and the return to the pristine Islam of the Salaf, and the purifying of Islamic culture from Western and Shi'a influences through armed *jihad*. It is this reinterpretation that has blurred the text from its interpretation.

The reactions of those supporting Hamas need to be understood as cognitive-dissonance reduction. This requires vilifying the victim to uphold one's prejudices. This involves four theoretical paradigms of cognitive dissonance, the mental stress people experience when exposed to information that is inconsistent with their beliefs, ideals or values. The worst demonisation of the Jewish state has typically followed the worst atrocities against it. They have failed to recognise the Hamas cult of hate and death of the 'other'. They are cowards who use civilians, especially women and children, as shields. They use holy places for their radical evil activities, which negates the purpose of any peaceful religion. It is time that all the countries that claim to be peaceful and modern spoke against these fascist terror groups. The Palestinian Resistance has been hijacked by fascist terror with a religious adjective, 'political *jihad*'. It vows annihilation of the other, whom they term as faithless and a lie. This is nothing but dehumanisation and de-secularisation of the Palestinian campaign. It is also a perversion of martyrdom and a rejection of human life that combines rage with hatred and senseless killing. It is time the civilized world speak for order instead of terror. Finally, the words of W.B. Yeats, which bring out the moral dilemmas of the present extremely divided and polarised world:

Things fall apart; the centre cannot hold;
Mere anarchy is loosed upon the world;
The blood dimmed tide is loosed, and everywhere
The ceremony of innocence is drowned;
The best lack all conviction, while the worst
Are full of passionate intensity.

42

Terrorism as an Instrument of Foreign Policy

The recent terror attacks on the fiftieth anniversary of the Yom Kippur war by Hamas aided with Hezbollah, and supported by Iran, are a dangerous signal. It displays the cowardice of attacking unarmed civilians, raping women and killing children and filming this savagery for to show it to the world. Which religion permits this? Whatever the cause no one can legitimise these actions. One is shocked all this is being done in the name of people who are the silent majority, who in their wildest dreams, do not support. Terrorists are those who cannot win in a democratic process, hence, they want to dominate through fear of untold violence. They are savages and it is necessary for all the civilised world to condemn such hate and violence against people who are different and diverse. Terrorists are averse to a democracy where they will be held accountable; they would rather hijack a religion to legitimise their plunder, looting, rape and savagery.

Terrorism as a state tool involves the intentional use of violence or the threat of violence to achieve political objectives. It transcends borders and encompasses a spectrum of tactics, from proxy warfare to covert operations. The moral dilemma arises from the stark contrast between international condemnation of terrorism and states' pragmatic pursuit of strategic goals. States depict vast hypocrisy as they condemn terrorism in rhetoric while engaging in covert support for such activities. There are unintended consequences. Historical examples showcase instances where states, in supporting terrorism, faced unintended consequences, including blowback and instability. Pakistan is a prime example; it sought to destabilise and terrorise India and its populace by fostering support for and actively funding terror groups but now bears the brunt of terrorism.

What are the motivations behind state-sponsored terrorism? It is an eye-opener for all democracies when countries like Pakistan, Qatar, Canada, and Iran sponsor or give refuge to terror. National interests include expanding geopolitical influence, the quest for regional dominance, and the protection of economic or security concerns that prompt states to engage in sponsoring terrorism. It is effectively a war by other means. Moral considerations often take a back seat when states prioritise strategic objectives. Morality in international relations is lopsided and often gets overshadowed when hard realities come into play.

Hence, do-gooder states that show moral repugnance towards terrorism are, ironically, found to support it when they see an opportunity to use terrorism for their benefit. In other words, states find moral principles less attractive for perceived greater goods, such as power in global politics.

What is the reason that states support terrorism as an instrument of state policy? It is a low-cost affair with lucrative short-term gains. They can do anything, and the victim state should not retaliate. In this case, they have provided a legitimate rationale for the entire civilised world to come together. The economic appeal of supporting terrorism is unavoidable for many states, particularly given the precarious nature of the global economy, which remains fragile for a variety of reasons. And in such situations, terrorism is a cheap yet effective way to get what they want. States' belief in the short-term benefits of supporting terrorism is more prominent and prevalent despite the historical evidence of blowback. The covert nature of state-sponsored terrorism involves carefully orchestrated actions to maintain plausible deniability. Although it comes with risks and consequences, it remains an attractive option for states to sponsor terrorism.

Genocide and calls for it against an entire group must be condemned, as, Hamas or Hezbollah and their state sponsors have called for the extermination and annihilation of non-Muslims. These statements need to be condemned by the Muslim world as it is essential that such terror groups are not allowed to have free rein to spread such hatred in the name of their imagined world and universe. There are also double standards in the West. The long history of

Western involvement in state-sponsored terrorism illustrates how lucrative and alluring it can be. During the Cold War, the US and others actively supported the Mujahideen in Afghanistan to achieve strategic victory over the former Union of Soviet Socialist Republics. A detailed exploration of the Iranian regime's use of proxies in various Middle Eastern countries showcases how dependent some states have become on supporting terrorism as part of their foreign policy agenda. And now the so-called Wokes support *jihadi* terror which sends signals of hypocrisy and duplicity.

There are challenges to combating such faceless, cowardly violence and brutality. The first and foremost is the challenge of an accepted definition, as one man's terrorist is another person's revolutionary. The danger lies in the level of brutality and savagery. Which religion and civilised society will support this? One is shocked to see support being given in the name of the identity of the terrorists. The lack of a universally accepted definition of terrorism complicates efforts to combat state-sponsored glorification of untold terrorism. Proposing potential frameworks for clearer definitions and the challenges in achieving consensus would be a necessary yet very challenging task. The competitive nature of international relations exacerbates the prevalence of state-sponsored terrorism. Furthermore, the unevenness of power leads states to conclude that they cannot afford a direct war. Hence, terrorism seems a cheap, quick, and easy way to obtain strategic superiority.

What is the way forward for a polarised world? Is this a clash of civilizations coming back to haunt us? Are terrorists going to dictate the world order? Are there no universal values, or are they narrow, based on identity that is constructed? While it is acknowledged that supporting terrorism has become an expensive endeavour for states today, given the extensive counter-terrorism measures involving sanctions, isolation, and public condemnation, states persist in supporting terrorism. In the Cold War era, the use of terrorism by states be it Palestinian, Khalistani, or Mujahideen terrorism— was frequent and somewhat acceptable within the Cold War context which allowed for an ethos of 'anything and everything'. The phrase 'one man's terrorist is another man's freedom fighter' encapsulated this mindset. Such acceptance diminished post-Cold War as global fears, tensions, and competition reduced in international relations. Yet, there is a resurgence of states employing terrorism as a foreign policy tool, notably under the reprehensible practice of identity politics. Canada serves as a glaring example, where the government, in an attempt to appease Sikh voters, jeopardises decades of diplomatic cooperation by supporting Khalistani terrorism and promoting Hinduphobia.

43

Trudeau's Domestic Politics Masquerades as Foreign Policy

In a recent development in India-Canada relations, Canadian Prime Minister Justin Trudeau's statements have sparked diplomatic controversy that breached diplomatic decorum and indicated his immature leadership. Just to keep himself in power, he is ready to go to any lengths to appease terror and those involved in hate speech, human and drug trafficking. His choice of language and actions have jeopardised bilateral ties and the safety of Indians—especially Indian Hindus—currently residing in Canada. To gain insights into how Canada, traditionally a favoured foreign destination for Indians, became a source of anger and frustration, four key observations warrant attention.

First, Trudeau's hubris and romanticised commitment to Woke values of hate speech and Hinduphobia injure relations with India and expose his divisive politics—not only of domestic politics but also as a disruptive instrument of foreign policy. One can better understand Trudeau's actions in the context of his political career, which embraces identity politics and divisive policies. Trudeau has sought to promote what appears to be disingenuous empathy stemming from his ideological commitments toward Woke politics. His approach has frequently worsened divisions in Canada rather than solving them.

Whether one looks at his vaccine mandate or his handling of the trucker protests earlier this year, he leaves no room for doubt regarding the potential dangers and authoritarian tendencies accompanying far-left politics. Furthermore, it is essential to recognise that Trudeau and his supporters mistakenly and regularly conflate his persona as synonymous with Canada.

Second, Trudeau's approach illustrates how not to handle a diplomatic situation. The episode seemingly emerged following Trudeau's visit to India after the G20 Summit. His decision to present information regarding a still-investigated killing, where crucial facts remain elusive—within Parliament was both deplorable and irresponsible. The utilisation of terms like 'credible allegations' and 'potential link' to implicate the Indian government without providing evidence or engaging in discussions with Indian representatives demonstrated not only an immature approach to this sensitive matter but also endangered the substantial Indian diaspora in Canada.

Canada is no longer a safe and prosperous nation with low crime rates. Instead, akin to many Western countries like France, and Germany, Canada faces growing concerns related to organised crime networks, hate crimes and anti-immigration sentiments against which Trudeau is not only ignorant but also ideologically blinded. For instance, the significant number of individuals involved in criminal activities who seek refuge in Canada under the guise of political asylum should have garnered the attention of the self-proclaimed proactive Prime Minister. However, his actions and policies remain misguided due to ideological bias, reflecting significant irresponsibility and a lack of diplomatic finesse.

Third, the episode shows how even developed countries externalise domestic issues by transforming a bilateral partner into an adversary for electoral gains. Trudeau's handling of the situation strongly suggests a primarily political motive driven by domestic concerns and a blunt pursuit of self-interest, illustrated vividly by his coddling of pro-Khalistan groups, notably Jagmeet Singh and his New Democratic Party. This must also be considered his waning popularity in his re-election campaign, poor handling of the economy and disparaged vaccination policy.

At this juncture, let's also analyse the allegations against India. Senior researcher and former Pentagon official Michael Rubin eloquently articulated two scenarios. First, if India was not involved, Trudeau acted without much foresight and damaged diplomatic relations that could take years to mend. Second, if substantial evidence points to Indian involvement, it would signify a grave lapse within Canada's security apparatus that harboured a known terrorist, a matter that India repeatedly urged it to address. Both of which demonstrate poor leadership by Prime Minister Trudeau.

Moreover, this also implies that the Trudeau government is not a reliable ally in the fight against organised crime and terrorism. Instead, it seems inclined to protect these elements under the guise of free speech. It is worth recalling that this is the same Trudeau government that introduced Bill C-16, which aimed to penalise certain forms of speech as legal offences without substantial evidence, potentially undermining the concept of free speech it professed to uphold.

Many observers of this incident have also speculated that Trudeau's sentiments may be linked to his perception of treatment during his visit to India. In all fairness, he was accorded respect and protocol due to a Head of State. When his plane encountered technical issues, India even extended the gracious offer to use the Air India One aircraft for his travel. However, any perceived snub that Trudeau and his supporters may have felt was largely of his own making. It is crucial to harken back to his previous visit to India in 2018, during which a dinner hosted by the Canadian High Commission in New Delhi extended an invitation to Sikh extremist Jaspal Atwal, who had been convicted of attempted murder. Extending such an invitation to a Sikh extremist for an embassy event in a foreign nation implies a calculated mischief designed to elicit sympathy and publicity from a particular voter base back home.

Fourthly, the incident illustrated India's mastery of diplomacy. India's response to Trudeau's politically motivated actions showcased a diplomatic masterclass. India effectively defended its position and presented its narrative in the face of Trudeau's assertive behaviour, demonstrating diplomacy at its best. This was further emphasised by the support from the US and the United Kingdom, as reports indicated that Canada had sought their help against India but was denied. The amicable interactions between India and other Western nations during the 78th UNGA session underscore this point.

Furthermore, India's response made it clear that it will not tolerate finger-wagging or condescending attitudes reminiscent of the Cold War era. It sends a strong message that the world order is evolving. Trudeau should consider this reality and rise beyond the notion of a 'White Man's Burden' to educate the Global South. Above all, Trudeau should understand that promoting supporters of terrorism, organised crime, and secessionist movements is something no government appreciates and is detrimental for an inclusive democracy. Any phobia cannot be legitimised, whether Islamic, Jewish or for that matter Hindu.

Ultimately, such irresponsible actions by the Canadian Prime Minister have yielded negative consequences for everyone. They have undermined the years of collaborative efforts and diplomacy and adversely impacted ordinary citizens, particularly India's sizable diaspora residing in Canada. This situation starkly revealed the hypocrisy and pretence inherent in Trudeau's professed inclusivity and social justice values. Essentially, it serves as a cautionary tale, highlighting how ideology and hubris can sorely damage the amicable relations between Canada and the largest democracy and emerging power in a highly polarised world.

44

G20 Summit Showed Civilisational Unity of Bharat

> "The roof of Peace rests upon the walls of Understanding"
>
> – Thiruvalluvar

Through the G20+1 the Delhi Declaration, Prime Minister Modi heralded a clarion call for *Vasudhaiva Kutumbakam* of one earth, one family, one future—a presidency of hope, harmony, peace and stability. But here in Bharat one saw a chilling testament constructed by the colonial discourse built by Bishop Robert Caldwell, a big mentor of the Dravidian Movement, who used his knowledge of Tamil grammar to further his agenda of his evangelical mission to convert the Tamils. The same arguments put forward by him have been repeated by a young dynast, Udhayanidhi, whose motto seems to be ignorance is bliss. What is surprising is the attempt to repeat the colonial and conversion mindset that still exists, and to try and insult a faith that is practised as a way of life by 80 per cent of the people of the state.

Is this a way to dent the cultural unity of this civilisational state that has entered the Fourth Industrial Revolution and declared its arrival on the world stage? The unity of ideas can be seen in that we have been one people, as reflected in the Sangam literature poem 192 in Purananuru, which gives a glimpse on the richness, maturity and wisdom of the urban culture of Tamilakam and beyond. 'Every city is your city, everyone is your kin'. This is by a people who for centuries followed a Hindu way of life. This colonial evangelical construct, being repeated by the neo-converts bring a dangerous conspiracy of creating a false reality that all other faiths are equal when none are. One agrees that the caste system is a social evil that exists among all South Asians, irrespective of faith. It needs to be eradicated, but not by spreading militant hatred.

The Keeladi excavations of the Vaigai River civilisation have challenged the so-called Aryan invasion, as well the Tamil-Sanskrit divide, thereby underlining the Dravidian-Aryan divide as an ideological construct. These excavations seem to predate the Indus Valley Civilisation and there is a similarity between the Tamil Brahmi and Indus Brahmi scripts. This substantiates the unity of this great civilisation. Initially, it was constructed with the purpose of the 19th Century evangelicals to convert during the time of Bishop Caldwell. Later it was used by the Dravidian Movement and the Dravidian political parties represented the latest post-colonial manifestation of the British colonial policy of divide and rule. Why are the same arguments constructed by Bishop Caldwell being repeated verbatim today? Are the same forces of divide-and-rule still at work owing to the failure to convert the majority in the state?

The revisionist attempts to use Caldwell's construct and mindset in free India will not work for vote bank politics. Their attempt to strip off Hindu practices in order to construct a so-called secular (in fact, an anti-Hindu) Dravidian Tamil identity seems to have failed. One such example at these continuous efforts is to depict the Hindu Tamil festival on *Makara Sankranti* as Tamil new year day failed, as the festival is closely rooted with the culture of the state. Likewise, attempts by international NGOs to ban *Jallikattu* also failed. *Jallikattu* is closely intertwined with Pongal and the farming community.

Are the Dravidian parties blindly following the colonial evangelical construct that failed to eliminate Hinduism or Sanatan Dharma as a way of life that has no beginning or end, unlike the Abrahamic faiths that are based on revelation and not through a process of evolution. Is it old wine in a new bottle to break this synergistic trinity of religious practices British colonial rule tried through divide and rule? They cleverly divided temple events into religious and secular functions. Then they usurped the secular functions from the temples, the centres of Hinduism to debilitate their social welfare contribution across India. Hindus are still grappling with reality and the hypocrisy of secularism in independent India, which has followed the post-colonial agenda of dividing and controlling the Hindus as the British did. It is hoped Bharat will give up this hypocrisy and discrimination and create a true *Amrit Kaal* for the 80 per cent at both the levels of de facto and de jure.

Now, let us put together the facts that the divisive construction of Bishop Caldwell was done to divide and rule. Conversion was a major agenda. To further this, Caldwell constructed the divisive narrative based on Brahmins as Aryans, depicting them as ethnically foreign invaders who ruled over the low caste indigenous Dravidians who are religiously different from high-caste Brahmins. Caldwell cloaked his conversion and divisive agenda with his unmatched scholarship of the Tamil language. He invented a new identity by coining the term 'Dravidian' in his groundbreaking work, *A Comparative Grammar of the Dravidian or South Indian Family of Languages*, that paved the way for a new assertion of the superiority of Tamil, independent of Sanskrit; this agenda-driven narrative inspired and continues to inspire the Dravidian movement and its parties.

Does the Church of South India adhere to the same construct by Bishop Caldwell, who, as a Christian missionary sought to prove the superiority of the Western civilisation as a White man's duty? Hinduism, or *Sanatan Dharma* (Eternal Order), has always been a fragmented, federated religion that allowed local communities to develop and maintain their own sets of gods, agamas, rituals, customs and worship patterns. Tamil Hindu culture is no different. Hindu society was organised around local temples, with spirituality, social welfare and social practices interwoven together.

The symbol of Lord Shiva as Nataraja as the main symbol at the Bharat Mandapam, where the recent G20 summit was held, brings in this unity and continuity of our unbroken civilisation. Shiva's dance has three significances, aptly brought out at the G20—the oneness of one earth, one family and one future. It is the image of Nataraja's rhythmic play as the source of all movement within the cosmos, which is represented by the arch. The purpose of his dance is to release the countless souls of human beings from the snare of illusion. The place of the dance, Chidambaram, the centre of the universe, resides in the heart of every Hindu or *Sanatani* (who follows Sanatan Dharma).

The philosophical dimensions of Shiva's dance, stand at the *Amrit Kaal* of Bharat, interpreting the icon of Nataraja as the perfect combination of the mystical, philosophical and aesthetic aspects of Indian culture. The dance of

Shiva relates to its cosmic significance, symbolising the creation, maintenance and destruction of the universe and ultimately its rejuvenation. All this is symbolic of what the G20 has achieved attempting to rejuvenate a polarised and divided world towards consensus. It is the signifier of cosmic activity envisaged in the five aspects *pancakritya—srishti* (creation), *sthiti* (maintenance), *samhara* (destruction), *tirobhava* (concealment) and *anugraha* (grace).

This symbol of Shiva as Nataraja bears the greatest of His names, Lord of Dancers or King of Actors. At the G20, this symbol of the Hindu civilisation that the cosmos signifies His theatre and He himself is the Actor and the Audience. The Lord of Tillai's court performs this mystic dance and the *Unmai Vilakkam* (The Explanation of Truth), verse 36 tells us, "Creation arises from the drum; protection from the hands of hope; the foot held aloft bestows release." What Shiva creates is the manifest and unmanifest world; what He destroys are the illusory bonds that fetter not only the world at large, but every individual soul in the cosmos.

All this truly symbolises the renewed spirit of Prime Minister Modi and a new confident, inclusive and confident Bharat.

45

International NGOs Interfere, Set Agendas Globally

Just as Prime Minister Narendra Modi embarked on his second state visit to the US, Cable News Network aired an interview with former US President Barack Obama. In the interview with seasoned host Christiane Amanpour, who has her share of hypocrisies, Obama questioned India's credentials as a democracy. Ironically, Obama hosted Prime Minister Modi not so long ago during his first state visit to the US. The host could have asked Obama why he did not raise his concerns about democracy while he was in the White House, or asked questions about the US democracy after the 2020 elections and the consequent January 6 US Capitol attack. Sadly, the references to US democracy did not invoke such apprehensions in the former President's comments.

Unsurprisingly, the incident caused controversy in the bilateral relations and embarrassment to the host, President Joe Biden. Yet, what needs to be understood about Obama's references to the health of India's democracy is that he was representing the viewpoint peddled by a complex global ecosystem, where the international non-governmental organisations (INGOs) (like V-Dem Institute's Democracy Report) play a central role. This is not to suggest that the former President should be absolved for making such distasteful comments, but there is a more significant problem that warrants attention.

The domain of international relations changed rapidly after the Cold War. Globalisation and the 'Third Wave of Democracy' led to the rise of non-state actors like media, multinational corporations, and INGOs. These non-state actors proliferated in the 1990s across all domains of international politics. Let's direct our attention to INGOs. But what exactly are they? Simply put, an international non-governmental organisation (INGO) is an independent entity that operates beyond the influence of governments, typically centred around specific issues, (or sets of issues) and carries out advocacy, provides services, and does what it calls educating the world about the importance and relevance of their preferred agenda.

'Religious Freedom' is interesting to understand the duplicity of works and what happens when a state sponsors a particular narrative or idea. Since its inception, the report has been a brilliant instrument of the US' foreign policy coercion that invokes the report when it is 'politically convenient'. The reports are predisposed in favour of Christian minorities throughout the world while remaining pliant on conversion to Christianity. Recent reports on India have been particularly critical, leading the government to publicly denounce them as biased'. The 2022 report expresses great concerns about the anti-conversion laws in India, allowing the Wokes justification to selectively present the values of secularism as a higher morality that is beyond criticism or scrutiny.

Judging those who are different from the Abrahamic faiths has been very confusing for those who reduce everything to one book and one God. This diversity and complexity go against the Western concept of order. For them, control and order are vital. In Dharmic religions, complexity and chaos are part of evolution and progress. They differ from Abrahamic traditions fundamentally in their approaches to knowing the Divine. Dharmic paths like Hinduism, Buddhism, Jainism, and others have developed an extensive range of inner sciences and experimental technologies called '*Adhyatma Vidya* (Spiritual Science)'" to access divinity and higher states of consciousness.'

Indeed, INGOs are extraordinary institutions that work as watchdogs against governments worldwide to address critical issues like democracy, human rights, religious freedom, poverty, and the environment. Different INGOs have made meaningful impacts on the global stage, with tangible outcomes for people on the ground. Yet, the role of these INGOs as civil society actors or non-profit entities has given rise to significant concerns over the years. Such concerns are borne out of their ever-expanding agenda, adherence to political correctness, allegiance to social justice, frequent use of flawed methodologies, biased approaches, opaqueness and unaccountability towards their funding or expenditure, and finally, a strong ideological disposition.

As such, one should ask how these supposedly non-political and non-governmental organisations are able to wield such significant influence over global affairs. The answer to this question is complex and goes beyond the scope of a single article. However, certain pathologies of international non-governmental organisations shed light on their appeal, influence, and modus operandi.

Firstly, there is the issue of indices and flawed methodologies. INGOs often publish several indices and rankings, such as the Freedom Index (published by Freedom House), the Democracy Index (published by V-Dem Institute), and the Press Freedom Index (published by Reporters Without Borders), to criticise countries that deviate from their ideological moorings. One should remember that these organisations rely on each other for content, validation, and most importantly, amplifying their agenda. The media plays a phenomenal role here. Take, for instance, these rankings. The media portrays them as badges of honour or shame, and failure to comply can lead to public defamation and isolation. This larger ecosystem reinforces these rankings through repeated coverage and discussions, creating a propaganda effect that treats them as undeniable truths.

To return to Obama's statements, indeed, he voiced his opinion, but it should be understood that it was based on inputs from the likes of the V-Dem Report which ranked India 108th in the Electoral Democracy Index. Interestingly, soon after the publication of the V-Dem report, major international news outlets, particularly those with a history of negative coverage of India, made this a headline story without questioning the intuitive contradiction: how is it possible that the world's largest democracy, where nearly 611 million people cast their votes in the last elections, ranks lower than countries like Tanzania, Bolivia, and Nigeria, which have a history of non-democratic rule? Yet, common sense is rarely common when one sees these reports.

Let's consider the Press Freedom Index, published by an international non-governmental organisation called Reporters Sans Frontières (RSF) or

Reporters Without Borders, in Paris. It's an example that may seem absurd. In its 2023 rankings, out of 180 countries listed in its report, India was ranked 161, well below Afghanistan, Pakistan, and Sudan. The interpretation of this ranking suggests that it is far more dangerous to be a journalist in India than in Afghanistan under Taliban rule, Sudan amidst civil war, or in Pakistan, which is experiencing a severe political crisis and has a history like the horrific kidnapping and killing of the US journalist Daniel Pearl. Ultimately, the unfortunate reality is that these organisations set vague and ever-changing standards, which remain elusive.

Secondly, international non-governmental organisations exhibit severe selectivity in their assessments and reports. With the same moral principle for which these organisations blame one country or government, they brazenly turn a blind eye to other countries or governments in support of their donors, investors, or ideological allies. For instance, the INGO Greenpeace tends to favour developed countries in climate discussions, demanding more from developing countries and accusing them of doing less. What is concerning here is that the failure to align with the organisations' ideological and political predispositions can result in unfavourable treatment. This means one country may be listed as a poor performer, without investments or economic opportunities. Consider the role of the Oxfam report (another INGO) in influencing investor confidence in a country that the report has censured. This cherry-picking of causes creates imbalances and pollutes the broader understanding of global challenges.

Thirdly, it is noteworthy that international non-governmental organisations (INGOs) often fall short of upholding the ideals of transparency and accountability, which they demand from governments worldwide. This raises concerns about their credibility, particularly regarding issues such as opaque funding sources and the transparency of how funds are utilised. These organizations are also disparaged for their high-handedness in their operations within developing and least-developed countries, as they insist on doing things their way without comprehending local conditions and environment. Additionally, there is unhealthy competition among different organisations, given their overlapping agendas, which is prominently observed in humanitarian and medical aid. Such concerns further undermine their credibility and effectiveness. Furthermore, there is a striking irony in these organisations criticising the government for their large bureaucratic structures and inefficient support staff. Prominent INGOs such as Greenpeace, Amnesty International, and Human Rights Watch now operate massive bureaucracies that humble many smaller nation-states. Like many others, this contradiction calls into question the effectiveness and efficiency of these organisations in achieving their stated goals.

In conclusion, former President Barack Obama's comments on Indian democracy shed light on the significant role played by international non-governmental organisations (INGOs) in shaping global affairs and the fractured boundaries between the Church and the State, as well as between the State and Civil society actors. The influence of INGOs, driven by flawed methodologies and biased scrutiny, raises concerns about their credibility. Additionally, the lack of transparency and accountability within INGOs, coupled with their own inefficiencies and bureaucratic structures, further undermines their effectiveness. While it is essential to recognise that some INGOs undertake commendable work with little or no compensation, the prevailing trend of politically intrusive international non-governmental organisations only erodes their credibility and leaves critical global political challenges unmitigated and unresolved. It is also an issue of hegemony of the West and dominance over others, whose cultures or civilisations they fail to understand or purposely try to demonise the other. Complex realities are oversimplified.

Icons

46

Strategic Genius: Shivaji's Contributions to Indian Defence

India Shivaji's diplomatic acumen in forging alliances with European powers like the Portuguese and the British had significant economic ramifications. These alliances facilitated the exchange of goods and technologies, stimulating trade and economic development. In particular, Shivaji's treaty with the British East India Company paved the way for the introduction of European weaponry and technologies, contributing to the modernisation of India's military and, by extension, its economy.

At a time when the significance of naval power was largely overlooked in India, Shivaji Maharaj had the foresight to recognise its vital role in both defence and offence. He laid the foundation of the Maratha naval force in 1654 near Kalyan and went on to build multiple fortified naval bases along the western coastline. His fleet, a blend of various types of ships commanded by a mix of local and foreign expertise, was a testament to his visionary leadership.

Employing innovative tactics like guerrilla warfare at sea, hand-to-hand combat, and strategic fleet positioning, he defended the Maratha territory against foreign invasions and used his naval strength for diplomatic leverage. His naval endeavours laid the groundwork for India's future maritime operations and continue to inspire naval strategy in modern times. Shivaji Maharaj is rightfully celebrated for these groundbreaking contributions as the Father of the Indian Navy, encapsulating his enduring maritime legacy.

Inhibiting History

In a 2015 piece in the *Hindustan Times*, historian Ramachandra Guha minimised the contributions of the Marathas, including Shivaji and Rana Pratap, by labelling them 'essentially regional figures'. Adding insult to injury, he claimed these figures practised 'feudalism', endorsed 'caste hierarchies', and upheld 'scriptural and social practices which led to the subordination of women'. Left-leaning historians often speak of inclusivity, contextual understanding, and caution against generalising when discussing Aurangzeb. Yet, these cautions fade when they discuss figures like Shivaji, Ranjit Singh, and Rana Pratap.

When discussing Shivaji and his political and military life, the inevitable mention of figures like Afzal Khan and Aurangzeb underscores his significance as a national figure. If these contributions do not warrant a national discussion, it is difficult to understand what does. By the same logic, one could argue that the Mughals should be studied only as north Indian rulers, regardless of their southern expansions. After all, they ruled from Delhi and spent their time in north India, making their southern conquests merely a sidenote.

Strategic Visionary

The context of Shivaji's achievements lends them even more value, considering that during his time, India was deeply divided along religious and caste lines. Under overarching Muslim rule, Hindus suffered under feudal policies, religious persecution, and stagnant social mobility. For Hindus, the political, intellectual, and religious domains had shrunk so drastically in many parts of India that basic security and safety were no longer certain. Within this context, one should evaluate the contributions of Shivaji and the Marathas to our understanding of religious rights, practices, and national security.

With his sizeable standing cavalry, an extensive network of forts, and organised rank-and-file cadre, Shivaji maintained an effective military force that achieved significant success against much larger armies. This aspect of Shivaji, in particular, and the Marathas in general, remains underexplored. However, his vision for organising the security apparatus and strengthening military capabilities, especially diversifying into the naval domain, was indeed visionary.

Part of this vision is understood through the realities of that time, where Shivaji recognised the need for naval consolidation. His rule witnessed a notable expansion of fort construction around maritime bases. He sanctioned the construction of naval forts, including Vijaydurg, Sindhudurg, and Kolaba, between 1653 and 1680. Regarding maritime tactics, Shivaji deserves notable mention because of his attention to and development of naval power, which his contemporaries primarily ignored. His naval tactics in littoral waters and his famous naval raid on Basrur near Kundapura, in today's Karnataka, with nearly a hundred vessels of different kinds, all demonstrate his military aptitude.

Shivaji's recognition of the importance of a secure coastline led to the development of a strong fleet to guard the western Konkan coastline from the attacks of the Siddis, Afro-Indians allied with Deccani Sultans. Despite the significance of his naval campaigns, they have often been overshadowed by the focus on ground battles in history books. Additionally, the dominant narratives about the mega-naval capabilities of the Dutch, Portuguese, and British navies tend to eclipse the mention of naval campaigns during this period. Yet, recognition should be granted where it is due, and the Marathas' naval capability deserves mention for its development and excellence despite the formidable challenges posed by the Mughals and Europeans.

Repossessing Shivaji's Relevance

While it is unfortunate to see the historical contributions of figures such as Shivaji underappreciated in the context of the security domain, it is heartening to witness modern India recognising and honouring his legacy. Recent decisions by the Indian Navy reflect this shift. For instance, replacing the British-era ensign with one based on Shivaji's octagonal seal during the commissioning of INS Vikrant in Kochi is a move in the right direction. Furthermore, the 2023 decision of the Indian Navy to replace the epaulets on military uniforms with an octagonal shape encompassing the national Ashoka emblem is a commendable and fitting tribute to Shivaji's legacy. Besides these, the Indian Navy's station in Lonavala, which houses the prestigious Naval College of Engineering (affiliated with JNU), is named 'INS Shivaji'. Meanwhile, the shore-based logistics and administrative hub of the Western Naval Command in Mumbai is known as 'INS

Angre' in recognition of celebrated Maratha naval commander Kanhoji Angre.

Indians remember Shivaji as a warrior, hero, and great ruler, but he was also a brilliant tactician and strategic thinker. His contributions to security, military organisation and naval expansion laid the foundations for even more remarkable achievements by his Maratha successors. Despite this, his legacy as a strategic thinker has long been overlooked. The Government of Maharashtra has set up a Special Centre in honour of Chhatrapati Shivaji Maharaj in the 350th year of his coronation a Jawaharlal Nehru University to study the Marathas' contribution to the making of India's security discourses and narratives. These initiatives highlight the depth and diversity of India's historical narrative, showcasing figures like Shivaji, who played pivotal roles in shaping the nation's destiny.

47

Ahilyabai Holkar: Reformer, Cultural Patron and a Leader

On May 31, India honoured the 300th birth anniversary of Devi Ahilyabai Holkar, a visionary 18th century queen of Malwa whose life story continues to inspire. From her humble beginnings to her reign as an exemplary ruler, Ahilyabai's journey is marked by her unwavering dedication to education, governance, social reform, cultural patronage, and military leadership. Such an expansive portfolio renders her legacy exceptional. Reflective of a deep commitment to the welfare of her people and the preservation of cultural heritage, Ahilyabai remains a lesser-known figure in Indian history who illustrated the true essence of *Nari Shakti*. She carried the vision and mission of the Marathas of Hindavi Swaraj and fought all invaders who tried to destroy the civilisational culture of Bharat. She combined Dharma with industrialisation. Dharma is not a religion but a way of civilised life.

Uncommon Upbringing

Born into a modest family in 1724, Ahilyabai was one of the few women rulers in medieval India. Her father, Mankoji Shinde, defied the norms of the time by insisting that his daughter receive an education, a rarity for girls in that era. Her education not only empowered her but also set a precedent for the importance of female education in a predominantly patriarchal society.

Ahilyabai's ascent to power began with the death of her husband, Khande Rao, in the Battle of Kumbher in 1754. With the guidance and support of her father-in-law, Malhar Rao Holkar, Ahilyabai took up the mantle of leadership, mastering administrative and military strategies. Her reign from 1765 to 1795 is remembered as a period of remarkable stability and prosperity. Even Jawaharlal Nehru praised her rule and described it as "almost legendary as a period during which perfect order and good government prevailed, and the people prospered."

Despite continual threats from invaders, Ahilyabai displayed exceptional courage in defending her kingdom. Her leadership was not limited to standing on the sidelines; but leading the troops into battle, further accentuating through her strategic insight and bravery on the battlefield. Her efforts as a ruler sought to foster unity among Hindu rulers and promote peace and cooperation across the region. Ahilyabai's military prowess and determination ensured the security and stability of her Kingdom, making her a formidable figure in a male-dominated world.

Good Governance with Social Reforms

Ahilyabai's administration was characterised by her deep commitment to public welfare, which combined good governance with social reforms. She held daily public audiences, ensuring the personal address of grievances that afforded her unique exposure to the kingdom's concerns and priorities. Her policies were inclusive, aiming to uplift the marginalized sections of society, including landless farmers, tribal communities, and widows. Her social justice and welfare efforts were pioneering, promoting harmony, justice, and prosperity for all. Most notable among these was her battle against the practice of Sati.

Her empathy-oriented governance stands out in her administration, which endeared Ahilyabai to her people. She based her reign on the principles of Dharma and righteousness, focusing on impartial and swift justice. As a result, administration can be seen as a blend of compassion and efficiency, setting high standards for governance in her era.

As a successor of the Holkar family after her father-in-law's death, she embarked on numerous projects aimed at societal betterment, especially focused on agricultural development, water management, and education. Her numerous charitable works, including constructing temples, ghats, wells, and educational institutions, were spread across the Indian subcontinent. Moreover, infrastructural initiatives, such as building roads and improving trade routes, were critical outcomes of her reign. Such efforts manifested in the transformation of Maheshwar (the capital of the Holkar kingdom from 1766 to 1818) into a centre of trade and industry.

Cultural Patronage and Religious Contributions

Under Ahilyabai's patronage, the city of Maheshwar flourished as a hub of literature, music, art, and industry. She established the famous Maheshwari sari textile industry, transforming Maheshwar into a thriving commercial centre. The artisans, musicians, and scholars were provided with patronage, resulting in a vibrant cultural environment, even while other kingdoms in contemporary India struggled to maintain stability.

Her contributions to religious and cultural heritage were equally significant. Ahilyabai's contributions extended beyond her kingdom, as witnessed by her nationwide patronage of temples, particularly regarding the revival and renovation of many temples desecrated by invaders. Her efforts to revitalised ancient pilgrimage routes and sacred sites, reflecting a vision that respected and revered India's spiritual heritage. She was also instrumental in restoring Hindu temples, many of which had been defiled by invaders. Notably, she rebuilt the Kashi Vishwanath temple in 1780, almost a century after its destruction by the Mughal emperor Aurangzeb. Her efforts at revitalising sacred sites across India earned her the revered title of 'Punya Shlok'. She also rebuilt the Somnath temple in 1782. She supported the construction and renovation of temples, ghats, wells, and educational institutions, reflecting her vision of preserving and promoting cultural and religious heritage.

Her Vision is Her Legacy

Her relevance to *Viksit Bharat* and the *Amrit Kaal* is the struggle for our factual history, where she deserves primacy of place as a cultural icon who fought against the invaders who tried to erase our memory and culture. Ahilaya's life and achievements continue to inspire generations, with a reign that stands as a testament to the potential of women in leadership roles, breaking the gender barriers. By advocating for female education, she exemplified India's progressiveness during the medieval period, where women's empowerment was on the least concerns of governance. Her leadership corresponds to the ideal of good governance that a ruler practicing Dharma should follow. The commitment to social justice and compassion as a philosophy of governance was, and remains an example of a holistic rule. For these reasons, Ahilyabai's legacy should not be viewed as merely a historical account but as a powerful narrative of empowerment, social justice, and cultural preservation.

As we celebrate the 300th birth anniversary of Punya Shlok Devi Ahilyabai Holkar, Indians should embrace her ideals rooted in simplicity, moral fortitude, and ethics. The lack of recognition that Ahilyabai Holkar and the significant contribution of the Marathas received in history is disheartening. Certainly, the way she broke gender barriers at a time when women had no agency should make her an icon of feminist scholarship. Yet, her mentions in history books or feminist scholarship are scant and still overlook her governance and military achievements. The most faithful tribute to Ahilyabai Holkar, the *Sivakamini, karma yogini* and *lokmata*, is to celebrate and disseminate her contributions to girls' education, cultural revival, and good governance.

48

Savarkar, Unsung Hero, Nationalist and Intellectual

Veer Savarkar was a multidimensional personality—a freedom fighter, social reformer, writer, poet, historian, political leader and philosopher combined. On 28 May, we celebrate his 141st birth anniversary. On this occasion, we need to understand why a scientific humanist and a crusader against social evils, like caste and entry of Dalits into temples through his Patit Pavan Sanghatana has been called a fundamentalist and a coward. A great social reformer who believes that the rigid caste system 'deserves to be thrown into the dustbins of history'. The greatest conspiracy of post Independent Nehruvian state framed him and branded him as communal and a fundamentalist when the fact that he was an agnostic who gave weekly lectures in Pune on "Is there a God?" He condemned all religions; hence the Nehruvian secularists condemned him, as for them secularism primarily targets Hindus and not the Abrahamic faiths. It is time that his contributions be assessed and celebrated.

Intellectual Nationalist

Savarkar's works and actions epitomise the true definition of nationalism, standing resilient in the face of adversity and continuing his fight against British imperialism. Born and raised in Maharashtra, Savarkar exhibited his distaste for colonial rule during his early youth, including his time at Ferguson College in Pune. Through his skills and hard work, he secured the prestigious Shivaji Scholarship, which allowed him to go to Britain, where he began contributing to the independence struggle through various avenues, including the India House and the Free India Society.

His capture by the British on charges of sedition, his struggle in the Permanent Court of Arbitration, and his return to India as a prisoner marked the beginning of his long struggles. These culminated in a prolonged phase of incarceration (1911-21) at Port Blair, referred to as 'Kala Pani' in the Andaman and Nicobar Islands.

The punishment was disproportionate and among the harshest that could be rendered to any freedom fighter of that time. Despite these challenges, his will and persistence enabled him to return to mainland India, although restrictions on his activities remained. His intellectual journey in the early 1910s flourished in the 1920s and 30s.

Among his early works, one standout book was *The Indian War of Independence*, which provided an Indian narrative of the Revolt of 1857. This displeased the British Crown so much that it banned the book. One of the charges during his arrest was his possession of that book, among others. Savarkar's other significant works include *Essentials of Hindutva*, which laid the ideological foundation for his vision of a Hindu nation. Other writings include *Mopla*, *Hindurashtra Darshan* (Vision of a Hindu Nation), and *The Six Glorious Epochs of Indian History*, all collectively highlighting his contributions to the intellectual dimensions of India as it was to come and as it should aim to be. He was also a notable Marathi poet.

A Legacy Betrayed for So Long

Among his significant contributions was the Hindu Mahasabha, a unique testament to his maturity of political thought that addressed the question of 'What after Independence?' His views and actions extended beyond merely addressing British rule in India; they encompassed understanding and enabling the challenges of Indian society, including fighting casteism and divisions that had degraded the self-worth of India under the yoke of foreign Islamic rule and later imperialism. His efforts to revitalise Hindu culture were not isolated but had a significant long-term impact on the Indian psyche, the results of which are evident even today. One speaks of an Indian narrative or a *Bharatiya* view of the world. Meanwhile, Savarkar was one of the first to see beyond the Independence struggle and envision India as a nation long before it became one.

Yet, Savarkar's contributions and ideas were ignored and pilloried for short-term political benefits due to ideological devotions. This has led to a skewed understanding of his role and the broader spectrum of strategies employed in the struggle for India's Independence. This marginalisation continued even after Independence and well into the 21st century. Historians writing about Indian history have treated Savarkar harshly and prejudicially. Parochial interests were so influential and pervasive that his legacy was betrayed through wilful ignorance and outright omissions. Even today, efforts continue to paint the individual as a fringe ideologue with vast chunks of his career either caricatured or entirely omitted. It took a considerable amount of time before both the government and the public began to understand and recognise the efforts of this unique thinker and freedom fighter. His experiences in Cellular Jail are nothing short of a horror story. Yet, a large segment of India's youth remains oblivious to them.

Reading More of Savarkar

For such reasons, there is a veritable and urgent need to read more of Savarkar to raise awareness about his works, thoughts, sacrifices, and achievements so that the resilient spirit of Indian civilisation can be better understood. His character in the face of betrayal by his people should be a case study of his resilience and strength. Savarkar's steadfast dedication to India's freedom and intellectual contributions highlight his commitment to depth and the enduring relevance of his ideas. Recognising and disseminating his legacy is crucial for fostering a comprehensive understanding of India's struggle for independence and its rich intellectual heritage.

In a nutshell, Savarkar represents the ethos of Indian culture and civilisation, which is resilience, pragmatism, and open-mindedness. Despite being ignored, outcast, and persecuted, he remained steadfast in his commitment to the ideals of a united and proud India. It is rare to find an individual as holistic in thought, actions, and vision as Savarkar, even within the rich tapestry of India's great civilisation, which is replete with exceptional individuals. Savarkar's contributions were crucial during his time, and they are even more significant today as India stands poised to influence global outcomes. He was a great Marathi poet, and it is a tragedy for a civilisational state to condemn a great nationalist who sacrificed everything for the nation and fought for a casteless and rational scientific society. He was a scientific humanist and propagated inter-caste marriage. The left-liberal cabal turned Savarkar's contributions to doublespeak and false propaganda. His sacrifice and contribution to modern India were belittled. When no big Congress leader ever was sent to Kala Pani, can one ask why?

Veer Savarkar asked for nothing but got plenty in return from a nation ruled by many ungrateful and mediocre rulers. Veer Savarkar got indignities, insults and ridicule heaped on him by men and women who were not worth to be dust on his left toe. He faced every false charge, every indignity, every insult thrown his way with equanimity, and when his time came, he faced death too with equal stoicism, on his own terms, fasting his way out. How many leaders of Independent India can claim that?

49

Relevance of Lok Nayak JP Narayan and Sampoorna Kranti Today

Jayaprakash Narayan's Total Revolution represents a profound vision encompassing the individual, the state, and society. It signifies a radical transformation, not necessarily of our material conditions but of the moral character of individuals and institutions. While rooted in Gandhian philosophy, Total Revolution is a distinct set of ideas within the literature on political thought. It synthesises Gandhi's principles on socio-economic issues and adapts methods to the contemporary social, economic, and political realities, thereby asserting its identity and significance.

Total Revolution (*Sampoorna Kranti*)

At its core, Total Revolution embodies a holistic change process at both the individual and societal levels, primarily focusing on moral values, decentralisation of economic and political power, and advocacy for non-violent means to achieve virtuous ends. Jayaprakash Narayan (often called JP) introduced this concept during a movement in Patna in June 1974. Although the movement was initially issue-specific, JP, as a visionary, saw it as part of more extensive changes in Indian politics. He believed that only a Total Revolution, or Sampoorna Kranti, could address the country's urgent problems and bring about a distinctive change in society.

While the term 'Total Revolution' gained prominence in the mid-1970s, Narayan had advocated for the ideas associated with it since the mid-1940s, if not earlier. He emphasised the need for a social revolution that would not only change society's structure but also improve the character of its individuals'.

Despite limited attention, especially by leftist historians, who may overlook conservative thinkers like JP, his early influences from Marxist ideas evolved, incorporating Gandhian non-violence. Narayan's commitment to his convictions and ideals led him to practice what he preached and preach what he practised. Consequently, his ideas were constantly tested in practical situations, leading to alterations based on experience. JP's concept of Total Revolution encompasses seven components: social, economic, political, cultural, ideological, intellectual, educational, and spiritual. These components can be adapted and changed according to the context and setting. When viewed in the context of his other political views and ideas, Total Revolution becomes a method of reforming society and politics without causing disruption or creating tensions. Instead, it seeks to reconcile differences and bring about comprehensive change.

A Different Kind of Revolution

Firstly, Jayaprakash Narayan's concept of revolution diverges from traditional definitions, emphasising an intrinsic transformation within the individual, society, and the state. Unlike definitions that associate revolution with changes in leadership or violent actions, JP's view centres on non-violent means to challenge the status quo. This perspective is particularly significant given the historical association of revolution with violence, often an outcome of leftist movements that usually resulted in bloody revolutions. Moreover, Narayan's philosophy shifts the focus from class struggle and economic interests to moral choices, urging individuals to discern between good and evil, justice and injustice, and truth and untruth as the catalyst for revolution.

Secondly, JP's Total Revolution challenges the Western-centric view of democracy and political processes, advocating for an approach that prioritises societal integration and maximum individual participation. He critiques the Western model of democracy for its atomised view of society and its reliance on political parties as intermediaries, instead proposing a more decentralised and participatory form of governance. His vision encompasses greater decentralisation of power, alternative modes of election, and re-evaluation of the political and social landscape through a non-Western lens. By transcending existing traditional frameworks rooted in Western philosophy, Narayan's ideas offer a unique perspective on revolution and democracy, rooted in the Indian context and values.

Modern-Day Relevance

As outlined, Jayaprakash Narayan's ideas possess an intrinsic Indian character that delves into nuances rather than providing simplistic black-and-white answers. His criticisms of Western democratic styles and institutions are a case in point. For example, the recent V-Dem report, which sounded alarm bells about India's democracy being in danger, led to widespread echoes within Indian politics. This reflects a tendency in India to exalt and appreciate anything originating from the West, which, in JP's language, calls for a Total Revolution to challenge the belief in the invincibility of Western standards. This revolution should be followed by a re-exploration and better understanding of Indian knowledge systems, which hold a treasure trove of largely overlooked and under-credited political, economic, and social ideas. Such a Total Revolution can help shift the focus from worshipping Western standards to rediscovering our own.

Another aspect of JP's relevance today is his insistence on decentralising government and returning power to the people. Fortunately, this principle of decentralisation is evident in Prime Minister Narendra Modi's government, which has employed citizen-centric policies, even banking on technology to reach the most remote individuals. In doing so, this approach has resulted in the devolution of power at the local level and the empowerment of ordinary individuals. Today, we see ordinary citizens accessing and using the internet to check on government policies and plans, question delays or cross-check the progress of different projects. For such reasons, one might confidently say that India is on a trajectory where it is getting closer towards realising JP's ideas of a polity where common individuals matter, not selected elites.

Yet, a societal challenge India faces in many quarters of public and personal life is the inability to look past vested interests, leading to the legitimisation of casteism, gender-based discrimination, regional divides, and more. Therefore, there is a pressing need for a Total Revolution in organising our worldview. Instead of being parochial, we must strive for inclusivity, a distinguishing feature of India's long history. And lest we forget, JP envisioned a casteless and classless society. As such, we need to move beyond biases and stereotypes and bring about this change without violence, rooted in intrinsic values and a transformation from within.

50

How the Nehruvian State Tried to Cancel Ambedkar

We are celebrating 75 years of the Indian Republic and the Constitution of India, especially its greatest modern icon, Babasaheb Dr BR Ambedkar, his life and work. Reflecting on how the Nehruvian State treated him is indeed an eye-opener. Any objective observer might ask whether the Nehruvian State practiced cancel culture. It did when it came to Dr BR Ambedkar and many others. The reasons are numerous, as we learn from books about him, particularly Savita Ambedkar's autobiography, *Babasaheb: My Life with Dr BR Ambedkar*. It is heart-rending to read how the Congress and the Communists came together to manipulate the defeat of Babasaheb in the 1952 Lok Sabha elections from North Bombay. It took the seventh Prime Minister, Vishwanath Pratap Singh, to confer the Bharat Ratna in 1990 on Babasaheb. It took the Indian State 43 years after Independence and four decades after the establishment of the Indian Republic to honour the man who gave it all. This is indeed cancel culture of the Nehruvian State at its best.

Babasaheb did not fit the Congress-Left definition of secularism. For them and the Dravidian parties, only those who criticise Hindus are considered secular. Babasaheb did not fit that hegemonic definition of who is secular. Babasaheb was not only a strong critic of Hindus in his writings but was equally critical of all religions, especially Islam. He wrote, "The allegiance of a Muslim does not rest on his domicile in the country which is his, but on the faith to which he belongs. Islam can never allow a true Muslim to adopt India as his motherland and regard a Hindu as his kith and kin." This viewpoint was not acceptable to the Nehruvian State, and he had to be cancelled, for he was secular and an intellectual giant.

Another aspect that Babasaheb was critical of was the Congress and its role in uplifting the Dalits. The *What Congress and Gandhi Have Done to the Untouchables* is a book-length study of the politics of the Indian National Congress by Dr BR Ambedkar, first published in 1945. The book undertakes a detailed investigation of the results of the elections to the Provincial Legislatures, which took place in February 1937 under the Government of India Act 1935. Dr Ambedkar offers an insightful account of the lack of political privileges enjoyed by the Scheduled Caste candidates throughout the election in stark contrast to the powerful, bourgeois-dominated Congress party. The work also aims to dismantle the misconceived popularity of Mahatma Gandhi as a 'benefactor' of the Dalit population.

Dr Ambedkar challenged the pretensions of the Congress Party as fundamentally representative of a unified India that accords equal respect to all caste groups by citing the election results of 1937. According to Ambedkar, Gandhi's social ideal was based either on the model of the caste system or that of Varna. Throughout his career as a political activist championing the cause of the oppressed, Ambedkar remained strongly opposed to the victory of mysticism over pure reason. He straightforwardly advocated the emergence of modern machinery as tools that would liberate humanity from the brutish condition and open up a world of possibilities for those who have inhabited recesses of darkness and deprivation for the greater part of their lives.

The five reasons why Babasaheb resigned from the Prime Minister Nehru's Council of Ministers on 27 September 1951 were, one, the promises made by Prime Minister Nehru while handing him the responsibility of law minister included the planning department, which was not fulfilled, nor was he appointed to any committee of the Council of Ministers. Two, the government was indifferent to the question of the Dalits or their status. Three, his opposition to Nehru's handling of the Kashmir issue. Fourth, Nehru's faulty foreign policy, as he predicted India would end up with more enemies than friends. And five, Nehru did not live up to his word on the Hindu code bill. Babasaheb felt let down, for Nehru didn't show the enthusiasm and determination to get it passed.

The worst way to cancel a strong leader who is a formidable intellectual was to manipulate and defeat him in the 1952 Lok Sabha elections from the reserved constituency of North Bombay. The Congress made this a matter of prestige issue, and Prime Minister Nehru personally monitored the campaign through SK Patil and the communist leader Shripad A. Dange to see that an unknown Narayanrao Kajrolkar defeated Babasaheb. The Congress placed its reputation at stake and left no stone unturned. They played all the tricks of Congress and the Communists to defeat the Constitution maker and cancel his legacy. An inconsequential person who was no match in strength or ability managed to defeat the creator of India's Constitution by a narrow margin [Babasaheb received 123,576 votes against Kajrolkar, who got 137,950 votes]. In the defeat of Babasaheb, the Nehruvian hegemonic state, in no uncertain terms, stated that there was no place for critical, colossal scholarship, calibre or abilities. His role in modern India is unparalleled, yet he had to be cancelled by the hegemonic Nehruvian state.

The Nehruvian State and its cancel culture tried to supress all those who threatened their hegemony, and one such leader was Babasaheb BR Ambedkar, a legend who ultimately authored the book, *The Buddha and his Dhamma* and passed away in his sleep on 6 December 1956. However, no one could cancel him. He rose like a phoenix from the ashes of the Nehruvian State. As we celebrate 75 years of the Indian Republic, it is time for every Indian to strive to fulfil his dreams of a casteless and equitable society as enshrined in our Constitution, so that it become a reality for a truly inclusive and innovative *Viksit Bharat* in 2047.

51

Omission of Indian National Army (INA) and Netaji: A Tale of Political Expediency Over Historical Legacy

India is gearing up to celebrate the 127th birth anniversary of Netaji Subhas Chandra Bose (23 January 1897), a leader whose contribution to India's independence is central but unfortunately neglected. Equally important is the role of the Azad Hind Fauj or the Indian National Army, which fought against the might of the British Empire. The Nehruvian state dealt the INA fighters a very raw deal. We are also commemorating the 75th Republic Day, an occasion that serves as a moment for reflection and remembrance and a source of pride for every Indian. Every such occasion of national celebration provides an opportunity to honour our history and the sacrifices of the INA freedom fighters.

These fighters gave their all to fight militarily for India's freedom. In an interview with the BBC in February 1955, Babasaheb Ambedkar elucidated why the British left India in 1947. Subsequently, Clement Attlee agreed Netaji posed the toughest challenge the empire faced. Several defence and intelligence experts agreed, too. Ardhendu Bose has further substantiated this: "It was not Gandhi's peace movement that brought independence to India. The activities of the Azad Hind Fauj and Netaji brought independence to this country, and it was admitted by the then Prime Minister of England, Clement Richard Attlee."

While it is true that the victors often write history, the danger arises when the narrative is incomplete. An incomplete history breeds ignorance; more importantly, it disrespects and insults the sacrifices of those left behind. The history of India's Independence Movement is a grim tale of this reality and the dangers it brings. The omission of the INA and Subhas Chandra Bose's contributions is not just such perspective to prevail, which could lead to articulating an alternative vision. What unnerved opponents further was how receptive these ideas could be to the masses.

The Indian National Army's cardinal error was not just a strategic mistake but a but a wilful desecration of their memory and sacrifices. Despite the INA's remarkable achievements, post-independence India witnessed a deliberate sidelining of the INA and its charismatic leader, Subhas Chandra Bose. Disguised under the exigencies of nation-building and the imperative to forge a unified identity, their stories and successes were suppressed. Their narratives did not align with the chosen historical narratives that emphasised non-violence and political negotiation while eclipsing the significance of armed struggle and military prowess in securing freedom. As such, the exploits of the INA were relegated to the background as an inconvenient truth. Yet, why were the INA and Bose relegated to the peripheries of historical discourse? Bose's evident charisma and appeal caused apprehensions among the emerging post-British elites. However, attributing his influence solely to charisma and tactical skills would be an oversimplification.

The crux of the matter lay in the divergent vision of India held by Bose and his contemporaries compared to the ruling dispensation. It is well known that figures like Sardar Patel had a different vision, illustrated by the consolidation of unitary bodies into independent India into the Bharat we know today. However, like Bose, these voices were sidelined due to the fear that allowing INA, built by Subhas Chandra Bose on the broad framework given by Rash Behari Bose, was the military arm of the League. Although Mohan Singh had angered the Japanese Army Command through his actions, they eventually relented and allowed the formation of a second INA. Mohan Singh himself recommended Subhas Chandra Bose for the leadership role. His reputation as a committed nationalist was known to the Indian diaspora Southeast Asia and the Imperial Japanese Army. As such, they were more open to the idea of a nationalist army led by Subhas Chandra Bose. The activities of Subhas Chandra Bose in India forced the British authorities to imprison him, but he escaped and reached Berlin in 1941.

In essence, the apprehension surrounding the INA as a potent military force frightened opponents to condemn it through unfounded charges lacking both merit and moral grounds. The INA and Bose, among the masses, were given less attention so that the role of those in power afterwards could be glossed over while their role was cast out. The INA embodied another vital element of Indian ethos—the value of sacrifice for the nation, a sentiment deeply ingrained in the Indian military tradition. It seemed that there was a particular disdain for a robust sense of nationalism and military strength, a sentiment that the Nehru government ironically supported and admired in other countries across the globe.

What is more regrettable and condemnable than the sidelining of the INA is their post-independence treatment. The fact that the disrespect and persecution during the infamous Red Fort Trials were never revisited until recently highlights the deep-seated apprehensions within the post-British dispensation in honouring their legacy and contributions. The marginalisation of figures like those from the INA and Bose reflects a broader trend in post-independent India, where numerous revolutionaries and even historians who dared to tell their stories faced marginalisation. This alienation can be attributed to two primary factors.

Firstly, although celebrated in their villages and small towns with statues and busts, many local freedom fighters struggled to gain recognition beyond their immediate locales. Their sacrifices and contributions remained confined to the local narrative. Secondly, and more significantly, those who played prominent roles in the fight against the British often found themselves at odds with emerging power hierarchies post-independence. Whether due to their lack of homage towards the selected few or their open criticism of the ruling dispensation, these individuals were systematically sidelined, discarded, and sometimes even demonised.

The last decade has been a course correction and a resolute and unapologetic affirmation and acknowledgment of the contributions of INA, Subhas Chandra Bose, and many freedom fighters from Manipur to Kutch. The government's efforts have ensured that the sacrifices made by these individuals are finally receiving the long-overdue recognition they deserve. Even in his 'defeat', Netaji delivered a massive blow to the British rule in India. And then, when India needed him the most, he 'disappeared'. Today, as we reflect, one may feel solace in the realisation that this legacy and history are not entirely forgotten but are being revived and celebrated. It is necessary to get the Russian archives opened to know what happened to Netaji after 1945. The statue of Bose on Kartavya Path and the release of Netaji Papers stands as a testament to collective efforts to rectify historical oversights and foster a more comprehensive and inclusive narrative of India's struggle for independence.

52

Henry Kissinger: Academic and Diplomat

The most controversial US Secretary of State, Henry Kissinger, passed away last week. Kissinger celebrated his 100th birthday in May earlier this year and held the rare distinction of counselling successive American presidents since the 1960s. The statesman's legacy is larger than life and varies incredibly depending on whom one asks. He personified the American ideal during the turbulent Cold War era. His endeavours in fostering peace with the Soviet Union, evident in disarmament treaties and détente, resolving the Vietnam War (earning him a Nobel Peace Prize), and notably, the diplomatic opening to China, are hailed as achievements that positioned Washington advantageously in the Cold War. However, critics point to his flouting of international law, human rights abuses—especially in Cambodia—and the forceful manipulation of American power. As a result, Kissinger remains a controversial figure in international politics, leaving a lasting impact on how he navigated the complexities of his time.

A brilliant academic and professor who was a realist, many professors would aspire to be as powerful as he was, and many professional diplomats would love to have his academic brilliance and well-studied writings.

In the context of India, Kissinger's narrative was often tinged with negativity, primarily stemming from his role during the 1971 war with Pakistan. This conflict, a pivotal event in South Asian history, resulted in the creation of Bangladesh and significantly altered the regional power dynamics in India's favour for the subsequent three decades. The animosity towards

Kissinger in Indian strategic circles is multifaceted. The US decision to deploy the USS Enterprise in the Bay of Bengal was undeniably a source of tension and concern for India during that critical period, which is attributable to Kissinger. There is also the personal language of Kissinger aimed at Indians as a populace and against Indira Gandhi. Another source of resentment lies in the perception that he played a role in integrating China into the global community. Critics argue that Kissinger's policies allowed China to emerge as a formidable economic force on the world stage. As such, he is viewed as accountable for enabling China's partnership with the US that invariably left India on the sidelines vis-à-vis the US.

Therefore, the suspicion and disdain directed at Kissinger in Indian strategic circles are rooted in the belief that his actions ultimately undermined Indian interests. By fostering ties with China, Kissinger inadvertently contributed to a geopolitical landscape where India found itself in a precarious position vis-à-vis the United States. The repercussions of this perceived neglect continue to reverberate, shaping India's stance on global affairs and its diplomatic relationships.

Kissinger's enduring legacy casts a profound shadow over the annals of international politics. Whether one deems his actions virtuous or misguided, the repercussions are destined to echo across the corridors of global power for years to come. Despite dissenting voices that downplay his impact, a closer examination underscores the magnitude of his influence, especially in the ongoing discourse surrounding China's role in world affairs.

Detractors may dismiss the notion of Kissinger's far-reaching effects, but consider the contemporary conversations on China's ascendancy in global politics. The debate intensifies as analysts ponder the consequences of Kissinger's pivotal encounter with Mao Zedong. Speculation arises: Without that historic meeting with Mao, facilitated by Islamabad, would China wield the same geopolitical influence it does today? The implications extend to its ominous spectre over the South China Sea, China's expansive reach into the Indo-Pacific region, military interventions abroad, and the controversial Belt and Road Initiative.

While some may question the validity of such hypothetical scenarios, it is imperative to confront the reality before us. Embracing the principles of realism in international relations, Kissinger navigated the complex terrain of diplomacy with an unwavering commitment to perceiving things as they are. His application of realist theories in practical diplomatic scenarios has given rise to what is commonly known as realpolitik—a legacy that continues to shape the course of global affairs.

Acknowledging the negative impact of Kissinger's actions on India, especially during the 1971 war with Pakistan, is crucial. At the same time, it is important to recognise the nuances of Kissinger's approach and the strategic lessons embedded in his realpolitik philosophy. While his actions may have had detrimental consequences for India in certain instances, they also provide valuable insights into the pragmatic application of realpolitik—the pursuit of national interests through practical and realistic means.

Indeed, Kissinger's academic background plays a pivotal role in understanding the foundation of his approach, as highlighted in Niall Ferguson's book *Kissinger: 1923-1968: The Idealist*. The core tenet of Kissinger's scholarly and later policy endeavours revolves around the centrality of power in global politics. His emphasis on power dynamics underscores a realist perspective in which self-interest serves as a fundamental guiding principle for state actions.

Kissinger's academic and intellectual journey shaped his conviction that personal beliefs, ideologies, values, and moral considerations often take a back seat when dealing with intricate actors on the world stage. The pragmatic realisation that pursuing national interest is a driving force in international relations is a key takeaway from his academic insights. This perspective influenced his policymaking, where a clear-eyed understanding of power dynamics and the prioritisation of self-interest guided his approach to navigating the complexities of global politics.

Kissinger's pragmatic and calculated approach can serve as a valuable tool for India in navigating complex strategic matters, complementing the empathetic elements introduced by the Modi government. Whether addressing issues related to Hindus or facing scrutiny over citizenship policies, Kissinger's thoughts and ideas provide a framework for advancing national interests with a resolute focus.

Countries like Israel have successfully employed a similar approach by blacklisting, denying or even withdrawing investments from the groups and institutions associated with anti-Semitism, showcasing the efficacy of strategic assertiveness. In India, figures like K. Subramaniam have championed a mindset that places national interests as paramount, indifferent to sentimental considerations. Subramaniam's influence is particularly evident in shaping India's nuclear policy, a decision that defied conventional wisdom and mainstream opinions, including reservations from figures like Nehru.

In conclusion, while delving into the discourse on Kissinger provides insights into the complexities of statesmanship, it is essential to critically approach his practices in diplomacy and realpolitik. Adapting such strategies to India's diplomatic endeavours requires a nuanced understanding, acknowledging the need for a foreign policy that is both assertive and self-reliant. Striking a balance between pragmatism and a commitment to being a force for good in international politics is key as India charts its course on the global stage.

53

350th Year of Chhatrapati Shivaji's Coronation

The 350th year since the coronation of Chhatrapati Shivaji Maharaj is an occasion of great historical significance, offering an opportunity to reflect on the enduring legacy of the Marathas and Shivaji's vision of Hindavi Swaraj, or self-rule. This milestone invites us to delve into the rich historical fabric of the Marathas, exploring their military prowess, governance and leadership, cultural preservation, and relevance to the Indian security today. These unsung heroes and gaps in Indian history need to be filled. It is time for both the Central and State Governments to encourage research in higher education institutions.

The legacy of Shivaji continues to inspire generations of individuals and governments. As such, to commemorate this special anniversary, we should look back at the transformative period of his rule that shaped the course of Indian history and continues to resonate today, without attenuating the profound significance it holds.

Making Hard Choices

The rise of the Marathas under the leadership of Chhatrapati Shivaji Maharaj represented a seismic shift in Indian history. Their emergence as a formidable force challenged the hegemony of the Mughal Empire, ultimately leading to the establishment of Hindavi Swaraj. Hindavi Swaraj was a clarion call for self-rule against the Mughal and other invaders. The valour, guerrilla tactics, military strategy and construction of forts both inland and on the coast as part of their unique naval strategy in the Western Indian Ocean. The Marathas' military campaigns showcased their exceptional strategic insight and innovative tactics, resulting in significant victories against more powerful adversaries. They were a bulwark against the Islamic invasions in the South and saved the south from the plunder of temples, genocide and mass forced conversions.

Yet, what exemplifies Shivaji most is his proclivity to make hard choices as a tactician on the battlefield, as a ruler, and as an individual. Instead of choosing a life of comfort serving the feudal lords like many of his contemporaries, Shivaji took the road less travelled as he sought to fight for freedom. One of his ingenious strategies was to adopt a warfare approach characterised by guerrilla tactics, swift mobility, and effective use of terrain. He pioneered the concept of guerrilla warfare, using hit-and-run tactics, ambushes, and surprise attacks to weaken the powerful Mughal forces. Later, this was reflected in his successors' campaigns that adapted to the ever-changing battlefield conditions to challenge the established order. Furthermore, the Marathas under Shivaji ventured into naval warfare even while it was easier to raise armies. Indeed, the Marathas became skilled naval commanders known for their naval expeditions and for establishing a strong maritime presence along the Konkan and Malabar coasts. Their navy played a pivotal role in securing coastal regions, protecting trade routes, and challenging the dominance of European powers in the Indian Ocean. The Maratha Empire's territorial expansion and the subsequent weakening of the Mughal Empire laid the foundation for a significant power shift in India. Their rise opened up new avenues for regional powers, redefining the political landscape and heralding a new era of indigenous self-rule.

Lessons for Effective Governance

Many discussions on Shivaji's legacy focus on his military conquests, expeditions, and defiance of Mughal rule. However, Shivaji's vision of efficient governance, justice, and welfare was central to the Maratha legacy. He implemented a series of administrative reforms that laid the foundation for a well-rounded administration. The 'Ashta Pradhan', or the Council of Eight Ministers, exemplified Shivaji's emphasis on diverse perspectives and expertise in governance. Each minister represented a specific facet of governance, such as finance, defence, foreign affairs, and intelligence. This system ensured a comprehensive and inclusive approach to decision-making, facilitating effective governance and fostering a sense of accountability.

Shivaji's administration prioritised its subjects' welfare, implementing policies promoting social justice and economic prosperity. He emphasized the importance of local self-governance and empowered regional leaders to manage their territories autonomously. This approach decentralised power and effectively addressed local concerns and needs. Furthermore, Shivaji's administration emphasised meritocracy, where individuals were appointed based on their skills and abilities rather than their social status or birth. Such ideas may appear standard in today's day and age, but back then, they were radical. A direct outcome of such merit-based appointments was that Shivaji's administration represented one of the most inclusive administrations in medieval history. The Marathas' administrative reforms also extended to revenue administration, where they introduced a systematic land revenue system that emphasised equitable taxation. This system played a crucial role in stimulating agricultural production and economic growth, benefiting the state and its subjects. The significance of such tax reforms is difficult to grasp in today's context. To put it in context, the Marathas under Shivaji implemented a revenue system rooted in equitable taxation principle, while the overwhelming majority of the population in mainland India at the time suffered from discriminatory and predatory taxes like *Jiziya* (tax collected from non-Muslims) and *Bhutfarosi* (tax collected from idol worshippers). The Marathas' focus on governance and welfare continues to hold valuable lessons about an inclusive and equitable societal structure that serves all, not just the few.

Preserving Culture and Celebrating Diversity

Beyond military and administrative achievements, the Marathas were passionate patrons and preservers of cultural heritage. Shivaji's reign witnessed a flourishing of the arts, literature, and architecture, creating a rich cultural and intellectual milieu. The Marathas' patronage extended to poets, scholars, and artists who contributed significantly to Marathi literature, music, dance, and artistic traditions. Their support for regional languages and indigenous cultural expressions fostered a sense of pride and unity among diverse communities.

resulting in fostering an Indian culture that stood distinct from outside rulers from Central Asia.

The Marathas celebrated diversity, transcending divisions based on religion or caste. Shivaji promoted a pluralistic ethos that emphasised unity in the face of adversity. He recognised the importance of cultural identity and took significant steps to revive and promote Marathi culture, language, and traditions. Shivaji's patronage of Sanskrit and Marathi literature and the establishment of educational institutions nurtured a vibrant intellectual and cultural atmosphere in his kingdom. Interestingly, Shivaji changed the court language from Persian (traditionally the courtly language in the country) to Marathi. This change was accompanied by an emphasis on Hindu political and courtly customs and traditions, as evidenced by his official seal, which was in Sanskrit. Shivaji's love and admiration for Sanskrit were not limited to this; he commissioned a lexicon to replace Persian and Arabic words with their equivalents in Sanskrit. Shivaji sought to promote the use of Marathi and Sanskrit to foster a cultural and linguistic identity aligned with the Hindu heritage in his kingdom.

A champion of social emancipation and the architect of the Indian Constitution, Bhimrao Ambedkar was also inspired by Shivaji. The landmark legislation CK Bole Act that opened public spaces for Scheduled Communities and the subsequent Mahad Satyagraha (1927) underscores the importance of Shivaji as a social unifier in India that employed slogans such as 'Chhatrapati Shivaji Maharaj ki Jai!' Shivaji's ideals and approach to cultural preservation serve as a model for embracing diversity and nurturing a collective identity that transcends societal divisions.

Legacy of *Swarajya*

One of the earliest nationalists of the freedom movement in India, Dadabhai Naoroji, is often credited with bringing the word *swarajya* into the lexicon of the freedom struggle. Later, Lokmanya Bal Gangadhara Tilak popularised the term, echoing Shivaji's vision of self-rule. However, the term was first coined by Chhatrapati Shivaji in 1646 CE (to declare war against the Adil Shahi to win self-rule), making this one of the most invaluable contributions of Shivaji to the Indian independence struggle. Furthermore, Shivaji and his stories profoundly influenced Indian freedom fighters, thinkers, writers, poets, and the larger Indian consciousness. For instance, Shivaji's ideals inspired Tilak to start the Shivaji Utsav, which helped invigorate India's democratic processes and fostered a sense of national pride.

The term *Hindavi Swarajya* has helped shape contemporary India in ways that many Indians remain oblivious to. This concept, popularised by the visionary leader Chhatrapati Shivaji Maharaj, embodies a spiritual and inclusive vision beyond political independence. It represents the essence of a nation-state that cherishes its cultural heritage, upholds egalitarian values, and embraces diversity. Under the auspices of this concept, Shivaji aimed to break the barriers of social hierarchy, social stagnation, and exclusion, and laying down the foundation for a more equitable society. As such, the concept has been crucial in forming a national consciousness and even in nation-building itself. This understanding of Shivaji's *Hindavi Swarajya* was best exemplified by his rule and governance, where ideas of social inclusion and mobility were so advanced that they may humble many so-called modern societies of today.

The principles and values espoused by the Marathas and Hindavi Swaraj remain relevant in addressing modern-day challenges. In a rapidly changing world, there is a need for indigenous solutions; national pride and participatory governance are invaluable in navigating contemporary challenges. As such, Shivaji's commitment to self-determination, resistance against oppressive rule, and the promotion of inclusive and decentralised governance provide insights for individuals, societies, and governments grappling with questions of autonomy, identity, and development.

The supreme sacrifice of Sambhaji Maharaj, who was brutally tortured and killed in a gruesome manner by Aurangzeb for refusing to convert under duress and standing up for Hindavi Swaraj needs to be highlighted to fill the gaps of history. One may fashionably speak of Muslim genocide when there is none, but few address the facts of Hindu genocide throughout the medieval period. Hindu genocide occurred in the Kashmir valley as late as 1990. It is these strategic silences that need to be corrected, and the facts made public. One cannot normalise rape, looting, plunder and genocide. Let us remove the ghosts that have been constructed.

In commemorating the 350th anniversary of Chhatrapati Shivaji Maharaj's coronation, the most profound tribute lies in upholding and cherishing the enduring influence of the Marathas and Hindavi Swaraj on India and its people. Shivaji's concept of *swarajya* reverberates as an indomitable force within India's historical tapestry. Its multifaceted essence encompasses making hard choices to challenge the pressures of foreign invading powers, their fanatical tactics, and genocide of local population, effective governance, preserving cultural heritage, promoting diversity, and, most importantly, recognising the importance of self-rule. However, one must exercise caution to prevent these remarkable accomplishments and legacies from being confined to a mere annual commemoration or fleeting social media homage. Instead, they should be imbibed and internalised, for there exists no finer way to honour Shivaji's legacy than to assimilate his virtuous acts and values by incorporating them into our school and university curricula, as well as research.

Every state needs to have a factual history that instils genuine pride. History cannot exist on shaky and fabricated foundations. The practice of excluding and marginalising defeated societies needs to be contested. Hence Marathas who challenged the Mughals were marginalised. History is weaponised with glaring biases, such as the notion that Aurangzeb was generous and secular, whereas Marathas were communal for they fought for Hindavi Swaraj. This is based on interpretation rather than fact. We are sacrificing this at the altar of political calculations. One should not erase large chunks of history that eliminate the *Bharatiya* narratives. We need a plurality of voices and truth cannot be blamed. NEP 2020 is a historic document and framework where these glaring gaps in history need to be addressed loudly and clearly, where we celebrate our spirit of resilience and courage akin to that of the Marathas.

Index